A PLUME BOOK

THE POWER OF FEMALE FRIENDSHIP

PAUL DOBRANSKY, MD, is a board-certified psychiatrist, a former associate professor of psychiatry at the University of Colorado, a national speaker, and a business consultant. He has appeared on broadcast and cable television numerous times and in a wide variety of print publications, including *USA Today, Marie Claire, Cosmopolitan*, and *First for Women*. He is also the sex and dating columnist for *Maximum Fitness* magazine.

Visit his website: www.womenshappiness.com

The Power of
Female Friendship

How Your Circle of Friends
Shapes Your Life

Paul Dobransky, MD
with L. A. Stamford

A PLUME BOOK

PLUME
Published by the Penguin Group
Penguin Group (USA) Inc., 375 Hudson Street, New York, New York 10014,
U.S.A. • Penguin Group (Canada), 90 Eglinton Avenue East, Suite 700, Toronto,
Ontario, Canada M4P 2Y3 (a division of Pearson Penguin Canada Inc.) • Penguin
Books Ltd., 80 Strand, London WC2R 0RL, England • Penguin Ireland, 25 St.
Stephen's Green, Dublin 2, Ireland (a division of Penguin Books Ltd.) • Penguin
Group (Australia), 250 Camberwell Road, Camberwell, Victoria 3124, Australia
(a division of Pearson Australia Group Pty. Ltd.) • Penguin Books India Pvt. Ltd.,
11 Community Centre, Panchsheel Park, New Delhi – 110 017, India • Penguin
Group (NZ), 67 Apollo Drive, Rosedale, North Shore 0632, New Zealand
(a division of Pearson New Zealand Ltd.) • Penguin Books (South Africa) (Pty.)
Ltd., 24 Sturdee Avenue, Rosebank, Johannesburg 2196, South Africa

Penguin Books Ltd., Registered Offices: 80 Strand, London WC2R 0RL, England

First published by Plume, a member of Penguin Group (USA) Inc.

First printing, June 2008
10 9 8 7 6 5 4 3 2 1

LIBRARY OF CONGRESS CATALOGING-IN-PUBLICATION DATA

Dobransky, Paul.
    The power of female friendship : how your circle of friends shapes your life /
Paul Dobransky, with L.A. Stamford.
        p.   cm.
    "A Plume book."
    Includes bibliographical references.
    ISBN 978-0-452-28943-7
    1. Female friendship.   I. Stamford, L. A.   II. Title.
    BF575.F66D63   2008
    158.2'5082—dc22

                                                             2008002657

Printed in the United States of America
Set in Sabon and Gotham

Acknowledgments

Thanks to Peter Miller, Lou Aronica, Plume, Penguin, the Womenshappiness.com team, and all those who bring value, happiness, support, and love to others. You certainly have to me. May we continue to pass them forward.

For my friends, and all friends. May you find
that your happiness, your success, and your life
transform when you discover the only force
that was ever really underneath them all—
the power of friendship.

Contents

PART TWO: Putting the Psychology of Friendship to Work

Introduction

No love, no friendship, can cross the path of our destiny without leaving some mark on it forever.
— FRANCOIS MOCURIAC

CARLY AWOKE *to bleeping sounds, a dizzy head, and a blank ceiling. She had no idea where she was.*

I went out to put a letter in the mailbox. *That was the last thing she remembered clearly. She had a vague memory of a sharp pain and of someone carrying her somewhere. It was a blur of sensations.*

Then nothing.

Now here she lies, alone.

Carly had some trouble focusing, but she finally fixed on the white walls, the drawn curtain dividing the room, the television hanging from a metal mounting. A hospital. I'm in a hospital.

What happened to me?

Carly was no stranger to hardship. She and hardship were practically sisters. The two of you get awfully close when your father runs off on you at age six. When your mother then sinks into a pit of drug and alcohol abuse. When you drift from house to trailer to shelter to bathroom stall because of that. When your grandmother comes along to pull you out of this morass and bring you into the warm folds of home only to have her mind snatched by Alzheimer's a couple of years later. When you move around so much as a kid that you never learn to make friends or develop any long-term companions. No, hardship was more than her sister. It was her very identity.

Still, she'd never awakened in a hospital bed before. She was in her early forties, she ate well, and she didn't smoke or drink. What was this all about? It had to be because of that sharp pain—yes, there had been a pain in her chest.

"You're awake; that's great."

Carly turned to the voice and saw a slim, brown-haired woman in a white coat walking toward her. The woman smiled at Carly and said, "I'm Dr. Samuels."

"What am I doing here?"

"You had a heart attack, Carly. We had a few rough hours with you, but I think everything is under control."

Carly could barely comprehend the doctor's words. "A heart attack? How can that be? I'm too young for something like that and there's no history of heart disease in my family."

Dr. Samuels pursed her lips. "Heart disease isn't always hereditary. My guess is that you've been carrying around a lot of stress."

That didn't make much sense to Carly, either. She was a property manager and sometimes the problems piled up and things got tense, but she never felt overwhelmed. In fact, most of it was easy to deal with. She worked alone in her home office and connected with most of her tenants over the telephone. Actually, these days, she did most of her communicating through e-mail. She could go entire days without encountering another human being in person.

"I don't think that's it," Carly said to Dr. Samuels.

The doctor pulled up a chair and sat next to Carly's bed. "Stress can come from many sources. We are wondering if you have any family, or close friends."

Carly's eyes dropped. "My mother and father are . . . gone. My grandmother is in a nursing home."

"What about girlfriends or boyfriends?"

Carly shrugged. "Not really."

The doctor touched her on the arm. "There are many ways to protect yourself against heart disease. One of the best, though, is to maintain strong connections to other people."

No one had ever said anything like that to Carly before. She knew she was lonely at times. She thought, in fact, that she might have had bouts of depression over the years, spurred on by how much time she spent alone. If she were going to be honest with herself, she'd have to admit that she'd walled off her heart to others. However, she never thought that in protecting herself emotionally she might be causing herself harm—actual, physical harm.

"I don't know what to do," Carly said forlornly.

"Talking to a professional would help. There are people in this hospital who could do you a world of good."

Carly was about to respond when the curtain rustled. Through it came a woman with short, curly hair. The woman looked at Dr. Samuels, then at Carly, and said, "I'm sorry; I could come back."

Carly couldn't place the woman. Her face and manner were familiar, but something was off. Suddenly it dawned on her. This was her mail carrier! She hadn't recognized her right away out of uniform. Lily, right? Her name is Lily.

The two of them had made brief conversation over the past couple of years, when Lily had come to drop off packages. Lily had a huge smile and a boisterous manner, and she always brightened Carly's day for a few minutes. They'd talk about innocuous things like the weather or some local event, but Carly always felt energized afterward. She often thought about asking her in for a cup of coffee, but she knew that Lily was working and needed to get on her way.

But what is she doing here?

"That's okay," Dr. Samuels said. "Carly and I can continue our talk later. Why don't you come in and visit."

The doctor left and Lily sat down. Carly noticed that Lily had kind eyes. They exhibited concern and warmth.

Lily tilted her head toward a vase. "Did you like the flowers?"

Carly hadn't noticed them until now. "Are those from you?"

"Yes. I brought them when I came yesterday."

"You came yesterday as well?"

Lily grinned sheepishly. "Well, after our little adventure, I sort of felt involved."

Adventure? What is she talking about? What does being in the hospital have to do with my mail carrier?

Lily's expression changed. "You don't know what happened, do you?"

Carly was so confused that all she could do was shake her head slowly.

"I found you on your lawn near your mailbox. You had a letter in your hand—I mailed it, by the way—and you were just barely conscious. I called an ambulance and waited with you until it arrived."

Carly was stunned, not only because she didn't know that any of this had happened, but also because someone had gone out of her way like that for her. "Wow . . . thanks."

"Hey, I wouldn't want to lose my best postal buddy."

Carly managed a weak grin. "That's often the best part of my day. Opening bills, would you believe it? At least it's something from someone, which you can hold in your hand."

"You wouldn't believe how many people just grumble at you when you ring their doorbells. You're always nice to me. And you always thank me. Nobody does that."

Carly thought back on the many times they'd chatted. She really should have invited Lily in for coffee. "So does that mean if you found one of those other people on their lawns you would have just left them there?"

Lily wrinkled her nose. "Nah, I would have helped them too. But I wouldn't have brought them flowers afterward."

Lily stayed for nearly an hour. She and Carly talked about some of the things they'd discussed in their brief earlier exchanges, as well as many new things. Lily had been divorced a number of years back but had a teen son she adored. They cried together when Carly talked about her grandmother, Lily having lost a beloved aunt to Alzheimer's, too. In the end, Lily said she'd be back tomorrow and they made plans to get together for dinner when Carly left the hospital.

Dr. Samuels came in again as Lily was leaving. They smiled at each other in passing.

"She seems like a nice person," the doctor said when she and Carly were alone. "It's good to know you have someone to rely on if your family isn't around."

"She's great," Carly said brightly. "I guess she actually saved my life."

Dr. Samuels nodded sagely. "Maybe she's only just begun saving your life."

The Friendship Crisis and the Friendship Cure

In June 2006, Lisa Habib of WebMD reported on an alarming new study:

How many people are you really close to? Chances are, not as many as you might have been 20 years ago.

A new survey shows that most people's circle of confidants is on average about one person smaller now. And the percentage of people who say they have no one to confide in has now reached about 25%.

If this data is true, it means that women—who innately, instinctively need friends in order to feel a true sense of identity, safety, meaning, belonging, and femininity—have suffered a loss of as much as fifty percent of what makes up the core of any culture's social fabric: friendship.

We clearly cannot afford to do without this most valuable resource—cannot forsake it for a promotion; for a fleeting, lusty affair; for the sake of fame or fortune of any kind. Friendship is more valuable than any of these things. If you don't believe this already, I have a feeling you will soon. If it feels as if the decline of close, quality friendships is something beyond society's control—our fate—you are right. Yet the very special nature of feminine friendships offers society a cure for this. By making choices and taking charge of your changing destiny, you have the option to cultivate a richer life.

Friendships between women don't only have a profound influence on individual lives. Their feminine nature is the very core of a peaceful, prosperous society. And for that reason, feminine friendships deserve a term all their own, Friendship—the fabric of community alliances we will explore together, and a process that creates the very destiny of individual women's lives.

The Science of Friendship

There is only one prime "law" of success and happiness, and it may not be quite what you thought it was. The Stoic philosopher Epictetus observed this law, perhaps first and best, in the first century. Later Sigmund Freud identified it again. That law is:

Character is destiny.

Character is the system of active mental parts at work in our personality. Character combines the maturity of your decisions, your ability to set boundaries, your ethics, intuition, intellect, beliefs, goals, emotions, and thoughts into one package.

Most of us learn the ins and outs of character—how it grows or how it often fails us—through the stories of tragedy and heroism we experience in great films and literature. This is one of the reasons that public figures of character like Oprah Winfrey and Steven Spielberg champion books and films. Films and literature—stories—offer us ways to grow by example. Through them, we learn of the failings and victories of character by witnessing the stories of other people, inserting ourselves into their situations, and understanding what might happen to us if we were to act in the same ways. The best characters in novels or films are those who are psychologically flawed but who gradually mature and overcome those flaws.

The field of psychoanalysis offers the same lessons, but it is a pricey alternative. What I have attempted to do for you in my books is to take that complicated, expensive field of study and condense its most powerful features into a simple system of diagrams. With their help, your character—and therefore your destiny—might be as easy to understand as a boldfaced road map. Developing your character and directing it toward success and happiness might become as easy as following a recipe: *character is destiny*.

Imagine you were alone on a deserted island. What would it matter if you had mature character or not? What would your destiny be except to scavenge for food, live off the land and sea, and entertain yourself somehow with doodles you make in the sand? Without others around you, would any of this matter? Very little. You absolutely need others in order to grow. If you were isolated on an island, the quality of your character would be almost irrelevant. In life, your character matters most in terms of your connections, love, teamwork, and enjoyment of the company of others. Your destiny can only be manifest through the ways you conduct yourself with others, what you give them of yourself and receive back.

This, of course, is what friendship is, an invisible force that is real and emotional, thoughtful and potentially wise, entertaining, joyful, and full of love. Without it we have no training ground in which to work out our character, no winner's circle in which to celebrate it. Without friendship, we have no place to realize a destiny of success or happiness.

A wealth of research in the medical and social sciences clearly indicates—if you read between the lines—that our health, our minds, and our contributions to the world all depend on friendship. Friendship is ultimately a hidden system that stores, measures, cultivates, and puts human character to work through group dynamics; it is a field of energy that can better our lives or cause us disastrous consequences. There is no such thing as "neutral" when it comes to friendships. If they're not dynamic, they aren't really friendships at all.

We know that friendships are among the most important relationships any of us have. In fact, as you read this book you'll come to think that they might be the most important of all. What you probably didn't know is that there is a science behind what makes us friends. Understanding this science can help you make friends, build circles of friends, repair friendships, and even end those friendships that aren't right for you.

Friendship is based on having positive emotions, and emotion is a kind of energy, the kind of energy that runs our psyches. In "brain hardware" terms, chemical energy (mediated perhaps by such neurotransmitters as serotonin and dopamine) may actually account for the "chemistry" between friends.

Yet I deal more in "software" than the "hardware" of the brain. The emotional energy of friendship, like any energy in physics, chemical or otherwise, is not a thing you can hold in your hand or take a picture of; yet we know from physics that it operates by laws that are the same everywhere in the universe. The energy we call "emotion" is not exactly like the energy of fire, magnetism, or nuclear reactions because it takes a unique form and process in our brains. Yet like those other energies, it does have a kind of mathematics, a system we can understand and use. Carly, the woman in the story that opened this book, did not understand this system (largely because of tragic circumstances in her life), and that resulted in a lack of friendship that had near-disastrous implications for her.

Caring about friendships and wanting to know how they work may be something uniquely feminine. There is a reason for this. Our brains have three functional areas: the *reptilian brain* (our instinctual brain, our "gut"), the *mammalian brain* (our emotional brain, our "heart"), and the *higher brain* (our intellectual brain, our "mind").

Men and women are in fact "equal but different." We are just as capable intellectually and in our careers, in the emotional capacity to love and therefore form friendships, and in any of the more sophisticated social skills that involve politics, diplomacy, ethics, rights, boundaries, problem solving, and other higher brain functions. But down deep, in a feature of our psychology that I call *gender instincts*, we are markedly different.

After a century of advances in understanding the more sophisticated higher brain functions and the ways of repairing their effect on our emotions through such methods as cognitive behavior therapy, psychodynamic therapy, and positive psychology, we now owe a great debt to the evolutionary psychologists who are just starting to elucidate the "animal" side to our natures as humans—the deep and unconscious instincts that are, it appears, different in men and women. These new psychologists tell us that there are two driving forces in our instincts: the need to survive and the need to reproduce, to pass on our genes. Having spent so much of the last century focused on the survival part, we have not delved enough into the reproductive part, where men and women obviously differ.

This difference plays out in our psychology. Remember that I am talking about animal instincts in men and women, not lofty, higher brain things like the fact that both women and men can be top CEOs, astronauts, or presidents. I'm not talking here about the complexity of our identities as individuals. I'm talking about the instincts that women have in common only with other women and men have in common only with other men.

At this unconscious, hardwired, instinctual, reflex level, men are driven to independence, to territoriality, to reaching out into the world, to fighting to extend their territory outward, and to defend what they already have. Men's friendships have a unique nature because men's reptilian brains have certain instincts that drive them to seek rank above other men. Yet they also bond with each other through teamwork, by working toward goals that raise the rank of their team above that of other groups of men. Winning contests is a core driver of masculinity and its growth. Men's friendships thus give society competitive force marked by a need for dominance, "alpha dog" individualism, and a tendency to honor one person or group over others. You can see the effects of the male reptilian brain in sports marked by significant aggression; in war; in cold, calculated decisions in the workplace—like massive layoffs, firings, and benefit cutting for the survival of the company—or in the justice of a stiff punishment that fits an outrageous crime. This is not to say that only men are rugged individualists, accomplished athletes, ruthless managers, or fair but stern judges. It is to note the general instinctual nature of masculinity as carrying certain traits of hardness in the face of the distasteful, cold realities of life.

Likewise, femininity has unique core gender instincts: to gather, to process, to belong to a group, to seek safety, to conserve resources, to create, and to be the analyzers, operators, and maintainers of the quality of our relationships to each other. While both the masculine and feminine traits are necessary for a successful society, the special nature of feminine friendships is woven into the fabric of effective diplomacy and peace, whether between corporate departments, communities, or even whole nations. The instinct toward shared success rather than individual dominance is a reflex of femininity, and the harmony instinctually sought after in individual feminine friendships spreads out as a civilizing force holding together those companies, communities, and nations. What good is individual achievement—such as winning an argument or even a war—if the societal structure around the victory is crumbling? Men and women need each other to be complete. Society needs masculinity and femininity to be complete. Yet feminine friendships hold it all together. As we will soon explore, the symbolism in there being only one ancient Greek deity of friendship, Hestia—a goddess, female not male—attests to this.

If you were to imagine the women and men in an ancient tribe millennia ago, you would notice that they automatically took certain roles by instinct. Men would hunt and fight. Women would protect each other in the village, create a safe haven, a comfort in the wild, and attend to relationships.

This all had a purpose: women's lives (and therefore the lives of the children and even the men) were at risk without the strong connectedness women had with each other. Women needed an emotional ability to "read" the condition of others—a stranger who approached the village, the facial expression of a sick child who needed extra attention, the whereabouts of a "friend" who strayed too far from the confines of the village, to where the wild things were.

We have been evolving for millions of years, so none of these gender-determined instincts is very new. For millions of years' worth of reasons, women care about friendships in a different way than men do. Women want to know how friendships succeed, fail, and grow. They want to solve the mystery of this invisible force in our destiny. They want, need, and must belong to a group of friends. This is why the feminine need for friendship is so deep, so intense, and such a source of pleasure and pain. Once, long ago, before gated communities and security doors, friendships were the only thing of true value to us and the only thing that kept us alive in the threatening wild.

Today women face new challenges: rapid technological advancements in communication methods, careers often taking priority over the people in their lives, and the ever-later age at which they find committed love. Still, as technological and "civilized" as our society is today, women have no less of a need for friendship. In fact, they need it more in the face of these new challenges.

As Carly discovered, none of the problems of today's friendships are insurmountable. To address such problems, we are going to explore a system together, an easy mathematics and a simple geometry, as fun to learn as it is to look at a cartoon, take a magazine quiz, or chat with your girlfriends.

Much has been written about women's friendships—about their nurturing spirit, their healing and transformative powers, and about their ability to help you find your identity. However, almost nothing has been written from the perspective of a male scientist who wants to help you with friendships not just in an academic way but in a very personal one.

That's where I come in. Think of me as an older brother with a lot of degrees.

If you don't muster all the skills and tools of friendship you can, you may find in another twenty years that that one friend left per American woman has dropped to zero. It doesn't have to be that way. Friendship is simply the deep understanding of the nature of feminine friendships, how they enrich your life as a woman and how they contribute to a stable, peaceful world around you.

You can change your destiny and that of the social environment. This book will show you how and why.

PART ONE

Mastering the Skills
of Friendship

Chapter One

Making Friends

There is no hope of joy except in human relations.
—ANTOINE DE SAINT-EXUPÉRY

S ANDRA WAS *in her element. At twenty-five, this was her first "big moment" and it couldn't have gone better if a Hollywood screenwriter had composed it. Only six months earlier, she'd reached an important goal when she got a job at a major Chicago publicity firm. In her first meeting with one of the agency's largest clients, the cosmetic manufacturer Preen, she suggested they host a breast cancer fund-raiser. Her boss threw her a sidelong glance (she only later learned that Preen was notoriously tight when it came to charitable donations), but the marketing exec from Preen loved the idea and asked Sandra to arrange it. The last six weeks were a whirlwind of planning, but tonight it had all paid off—the event was a smash.*

Of course, Sandra had tapped into her large network of friends to help generate excitement and interest in the fund-raiser. As she strolled through the crowd to make sure that everyone was content, she waved to Karen from her book club, shared a couple of words with Jackie from her boyfriend's office, giggled as she watched Julie from her young executives' group work the room in expert fashion, and blew a kiss to Isabel from the Girls' Night Out group that Sandra started and that had now become a monthly social event throughout the city. Sandra was thrilled by how many of her friends had shown up and equally thrilled at the prospect of getting to know lots of others at this function. The music was great, the food was delicious, and the guest speaker was guaranteed to bring the audience new insights. This was monster publicity for Preen and, more important, a huge income generator for a critical cause.

As Sandra chatted with the Preen marketing associate who helped her with the event, Connie, Sandra's oldest and dearest friend, sidled up next to them. Sandra knew from Connie's expression that she had something intriguing to tell her. Connie's eyes always danced when she had something juicy to share. Sandra excused herself and turned to her best friend.

"You are not going to believe who's here," Connie said the second they were alone.

"Oprah? Oprah came? You know, I sent out the invitation, but I never thought—"

"Keep dreaming, babe. I'm not talking about Oprah. I'm talking about Tamaaaaahra."

Tamara? Sandra had no idea who Connie was talking about. Then it hit her. Like a sixteen-ton weight.

"Tamara Beauprez?" Sandra asked nervously.

"In the flesh."

"You have got to be kidding me. She . . . she can't mess this up for me."

Suddenly, Sandra's sense of feeling on top of the world evaporated. Instead, she was back in college, back to the days when she was a cerebral, socially awkward kid from the suburbs who felt like she was in over her head at Northwestern. In the second semester of her freshman year, she met Tamara at an improv class Sandra took to try to teach herself to loosen up. Tamara was everything Sandra wasn't. She was socially confident, fearless, extroverted— and fun. For some reason, Tamara made "a project" of Sandra and helped her bring out her latent abilities to connect with people.

They had a great couple of years together, but in their senior year Tamara turned on her. Sandra always believed that Tamara was jealous of how quickly she became adept at connecting with people and making meaningful friendships. Sandra tried to defuse this—even going so far as to tell Tamara that she never would have been able to be the person she'd become without Tamara's help. But nothing worked and things just got uglier. Tamara started hitting on Sandra's boyfriends and gossiping about her. She even undermined Sandra's bid to become president of their sorority. And all of it seemed to give Tamara a sick sense of satisfaction. By the end of that year, Sandra believed one of the great benefits of graduation was that she would never have to set eyes on Tamara Beauprez again.

But now she was here—at the most important professional event of Sandra's life so far.

"I have to deal with this," Sandra said firmly.

Connie grabbed her arm. "Why? There must be three hundred people here. Just ignore her."

"I can't ignore her. If I do and she does something awful, I'll feel like a complete idiot. Where is she?"

Connie pointed toward the back of the room and followed her there stride for stride. Sandra knew that, unlike Tamara, she could always count on Connie to stand next to her.

When Sandra first saw her, Tamara was facing the other way. As she got closer, though, Tamara turned. And two things struck Sandra simultaneously. The first was that Tamara looked worn down by life. Her clothes seemed shabby, her hair badly needed styling, and she had premature wrinkles on her face.

The other thing that hit Sandra was more shocking. When she looked into Tamara's eyes, she didn't see hostility or competitiveness. What she saw was friendship. She saw someone with whom she'd shared important things.

"Sandra?" Tamara said tentatively. "What are you doing here?"

"*I organized this event. I never expected to see you here.*"

Tamara smiled in a way that suggested she didn't use those muscles terribly often anymore. "*You organized this? Congratulations. You got a great turnout.*"

"*Thanks,*" Sandra said softly. She wasn't sure what to say after that.

Several seconds passed. Then Tamara dipped her head and said, "*I'm sorry.*"

"*What?*"

Tamara looked down at the ground and then made eye contact with Sandra. "*I promised myself if I ever saw you again that I would apologize for the way I treated you in our senior year. It was beyond unacceptable. There was just so much going on at once. More than you want to hear. The worst of it was that my mother was diagnosed with breast cancer. She had a horrible couple of years and then the disease beat her. I don't get out much these days, but I try to come to events like this on occasion.*"

Sandra felt her heart melting. "*I'm so sorry to hear about your mother. You should have told me back then.*"

"*I know I should have. I should have done a lot of things differently back then. I'm really sorry, Sandra.*"

Sandra reached out and took Tamara's hand. "*You're not leaving here without giving me your phone number. We have a lot of catching up to do.*"

Sandra came to the event that night expecting a professional triumph. What she got, however, was so much more.

Men, Women, and Friendship

When I developed the psychology model called mindOS™: the operating system of the human mind, one glaring concept about male-female differences came out. If we were to look at the mind as different from the brain and see it as a kind of software rather than a collection of specific anatomical bits of hardware, our understanding of psychology and the practical applications of it become exceedingly easy and elegant. Men and women are equal in potential for achieving mature character and its rewards but simply different in gender instincts.

In designing mindOS as a means of rapidly teaching the understanding of instinct and the growth of character, I came from no single "school" of psychology but rather used as many highly researched paradigms as I could find, synthesizing them into one model. The most recent of these is evolutionary psychology. If we go back several decades to Paul MacLean's innovative triune brain theory, we see something revolutionary in terms of viewing the general connection between brain and mind. The brain can be divided into three parts, each stacked upon the last, from the most primitive and animalistic to the most sophisticated, civilized, and uniquely human. MacLean called the three parts the reptilian brain, the mammalian brain, and the higher brain.

The reptilian brain is where all the human instincts, unconscious reflexes, and social strategies arise. Freud theorized about unconscious processes that work in us without our having to think about them, processes that deal with core human imperatives such as sexuality and survival. Freud coined the term *unconscious* and delineated certain universals at work in terms of our desire to escape our deepseated anxiety. Of course, the most anxiety-provoking experience you can think of is the threat of imminent death, which happened to be a far more common experience for ancient hunter-gatherers than it is today. Freud and his successors also addressed the nature of human sexuality, agreeing that there are differences in the strategies used by men and women in order to reproduce.

Evolutionary psychology also focuses on the core drives in our instinctual behavior to survive and reproduce. It is Charles Darwin's theory of natural selection revisited, not just in terms of physical

The Three Brains of a Potential Friend

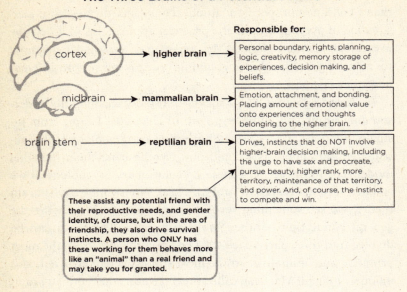

		Responsible for:
cortex	→ **higher brain** →	Personal boundary, rights, planning, logic, creativity, memory storage of experiences, decision making, and beliefs.
midbrain →	**mammalian brain** →	Emotion, attachment, and bonding. Placing amount of emotional value onto experiences and thoughts belonging to the higher brain.
brain stem →	**reptilian brain** →	Drives, instincts that do NOT involve higher-brain decision making, including the urge to have sex and procreate, pursue beauty, higher rank, more territory, maintenance of that territory, and power. And, of course, the instinct to compete and win.

These assist any potential friend with their reproductive needs, and gender identity, of course, but in the area of friendship, they also drive survival instincts. A person who ONLY has these working for them behaves more like an "animal" than a real friend and may take you for granted.

features such as our body's shape and function, but in terms of the function of our minds. Both Freud and the evolutionary psychologists were addressing the same thing with different metaphors: men and women are *equal* in their instinctual, unconscious, hardwired drive to survive (or at least to avoid the negative emotion called anxiety, the harbinger of impending death), but they are *different* in their strategies when it comes to the psychology of reproducing, of finding and bonding with a mate to have children.

The reptilian brain is the collection of all the human processes that are unconscious or reflex or instinct-based. Both men and women startle at a loud noise and panic when a wild animal is charging at them. These things operate in both sexes for one purpose: to keep us alive through anxiety by sending our bodies into action without thinking.

Yet there are instincts unique to women: breast-feeding a new-born, bonding with it in a style very different from a father's; connecting with other women in a very different way from how men relate to other men, a "gender instinct" to fit in or belong to social groups as opposed to the masculine gender instinct that drives rank-seeking among male groups; and the feminine gender instinct—driven by what is called the female Oedipal period of life—for finding interest in all things mysterious and wanting answers to even the small riddles of daily life. Men may have more of an instinctual bent toward taking action out in the world, rather than seeking harmony in the home. By instinct, I mean non-logic-based reflex—the animal part of our nature as opposed to the sophistications of human intelligence and mature character. Men are driven by a different set of reflexes than women: to seek solitude when contemplating solutions to challenges, to strive for goals in which one is the sole "winner," and to gain rank among other men by so doing.

If we package all that is universally the same about humans in a box we call the reptilian brain, we see all the instincts that helped us to survive in small, intimate groups of hunter-gatherers ages ago and that today come into play in the small, intimate groups we call *circles of friends*.

The reptilian brain makes men, men and women, women in our minds not just in our bodies. The reptilian brain also makes men and women different from each other.

There is much more to us, of course, than that animal nature of gender instincts. Just as the reptilian brain is like a primitive software program that runs all our instincts and shows us that the minds of men and women have differences, the mammalian brain is like a somewhat more advanced program that runs our emotions. Both men and women are equally gifted at having a capacity to love, since love is scientifically just the passing of positive emotion from one person to another. The reason that MacLean and the evolutionary psychologists call it the mammalian brain is that unlike snakes and lizards, which are almost all reflex in behavior, the higher animals called mammals have the capacity to feel emotion. A dog can be happy or sad. A cat can seem anxious or nervous, and today we even sometimes medicate our pets with Prozac for these mood problems.

Whether you are a cat or a human, you are a mammal. The mammalian brain, as the seat of joy, depression, confidence, anxiety, anger, self-esteem, and even love, is akin to the gasoline and oil tanks of the brain. It is the storehouse and processing plant for the human energy we call emotion. It is the center of what emotionally attracts us to others, whether man to wife, sibling to sibling, boss to new hire, or even a political candidate to the public. Underneath all of these kinds of social relationship is friendship—to greater or lesser degrees. The mammalian brain, then, is the area where the most powerful "software" of friendship lives in all of us.

The E = mc² of Psychology™

You have likely heard of Einstein's famous equation, $E = mc^2$. To physicists this equation is perhaps the most elegant and profound of this era. That's because for the very first time it explained the invisible nature of *energy* in terms of matter, the stuff we can actually hold in our hands and therefore harness and use.

In psychology, there couldn't be more important "stuff" for us to harness than *emotional energy*. I mean this in the most rigorously scientific of ways—not to be taken lightly or as pseudoscientific fluff. The energy quality of our emotions distinguishes our good moods from our mood disorders. It powers our mental ability to do work, to create, to calculate, to tell stories, to learn, and to grow. It powers our friendships and our very capacity to love. Wouldn't it then be remarkably useful for us to discover an equation that gives substance to what is invisible about emotional energy?

It would be the $E = mc^2$ of psychology, and I have just such an original discovery for you.

In my model, when we think of the positive emotional energy that exists in our relationships, what we're really referring to is our self-esteem. Every relationship "system" has a degree and quality of self-esteem to it, both contributed by individuals and as a collective whole. There are families with high self-esteem and low self-esteem, corporations with high self-esteem (we might call it morale) and low self-esteem, and married couples who, combined, have high self-esteem or low self-esteem. These levels of self-esteem correspond to the levels of positive human emotional energy present.

In physics, there are two general kinds of energy: potential energy stored in stationary, you might even say soothing or calm form (like petroleum oil), and kinetic energy that is actively spent to do work (like gasoline). In my psychological model, the positive emotional energy metaphorically stored in the mammalian brain also takes two forms: nurturing (or motherly) emotional energy, which is like the oil of the mind, and action-prone (or fatherly) emotional energy, which is like the gasoline of the mind.

In easy everyday terms, dividing self-esteem into two parts simply means that:

Self-esteem = Well-being (nurturing energy) + Confidence (the energy of action, risk taking, change, and resistance to loss)

In the pages that follow, you are going to learn to manufacture these two parts of self-esteem in your own life as if by a simple recipe. That is the $E = mc^2$ of psychology: Self-esteem = Well-being + Confidence. You will be able to harness the power of friendship via the self-esteem of your character, to guarantee a destiny of happiness and success.

This process takes the invisible energy of the mind and for the first time labels, quantifies, and makes that mental energy practical for you to measure and use in your real, everyday life—just as $E = mc^2$ did for physicists who sought to make use of the energy in matter. Understanding this new theory of friendship makes mental energy akin to a physical thing you can hold in your hands and make practical. In fact, friendship is the singular vehicle by which developing character leads to positive results for your life.

"Quantum Psychology" and the Higher Brain

In quantum physics, a particle of matter can be generally described or labeled according to its frequency on a spectrum but at the same time it can be "pinpointed" at a specific location in space, too.

In my "quantum" version of psychology, the features of a person's character can be generally described or labeled, and yet their unique personality can be "pinpointed" as the specific constellation of those particular features. In my system, I have found it highly useful both to label people's general character impairments as they appear within the spectrum of possibilities and to place each character trait very specifically at a point on that spectrum. Throughout this book you will see all the wild and wonderful ways character and its vehicle of destiny—friendship—play out in spectrums representing different areas of our lives.

Friendship itself exists on a spectrum, and the quality of people we tend to call friends is distributed along that spectrum, anywhere from acquaintance through shopping friend, lunch friend, classmate friend, buddy, or good friend all the way up to best friend or even BFF (best friend forever).

Labeling friends in this way, while respecting their uniqueness in our lives, is where the power comes from in my quantum psychology. It can give us practical answers about how to fix problems without stripping our friends or ourselves of individuality. We can categorize—and therefore take helpful action—while also capturing the rich diversity of our lives.

Spectrum of Friendship Quality

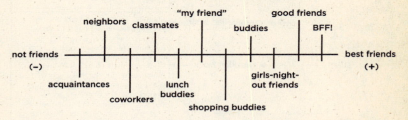

This spectrum parallels the degree of maturity of character and personal growth two people have reached, and to what extent they mutually share in that maturity. We tend to attract friends of a maturity level similar to our own. People are never the same "age" psychologically as they are outside, "biologically."

The higher brain is largely responsible for the diversity among people: their unique character, their level of maturity, and, of course, the quality of friendships they form.

The higher brain is the most sophisticated "software unit" of the brain. It is the very cause of the rise of civilization. The higher brain is the center of the intellect. It is responsible for all language and communication; our sense of rights, rules, art, creativity, and identity as individuals; the establishment of boundaries and limits; and, above all, it is the center of logical decision making. The higher brain takes care of what psychiatrists call "executive functions," the complex, calculating, consciously strategized processes. It is the area of the brain that makes each of us mentally unique, different from every other person on earth.

Think of these "three brains" each telling its own kind of story about our individual lives. The reptilian brain speaks of timeless myths and fables, the mammalian brain tells the Shakespearean

The Three Brains of a Potential Friend

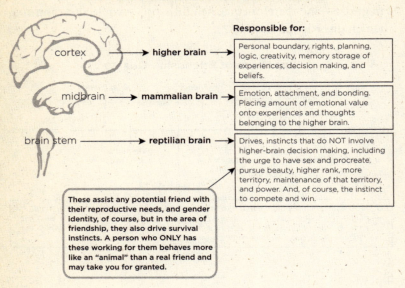

Responsible for:

cortex → **higher brain** →

Personal boundary, rights, planning, logic, creativity, memory storage of experiences, decision making, and beliefs.

midbrain → **mammalian brain** →

Emotion, attachment, and bonding. Placing amount of emotional value onto experiences and thoughts belonging to the higher brain.

brain stem → **reptilian brain** →

Drives, instincts that do NOT involve higher-brain decision making, including the urge to have sex and procreate, pursue beauty, higher rank, more territory, maintenance of that territory, and power. And, of course, the instinct to compete and win.

These assist any potential friend with their reproductive needs, and gender identity, of course, but in the area of friendship, they also drive survival instincts. A person who ONLY has these working for them behaves more like an "animal" than a real friend and may take you for granted.

dramas of humanity, and the higher brain weaves stories so individually detailed, so personally you, that it is like a little-known independent filmmaker who shows her unique, quirky, but compelling tales to small audiences, some of whom will become raving fans. These aficionados of the indie film of your life will be your best friends. If you were to learn about all three of these brains and how they color your friendships (with all the subtle and special differences women have within these life-saving connections), you'd become the master dramatist of your life—and therefore a master of friendship.

Armed with this system of friendship, you can solve each and every friendship problem that comes your way and, ultimately, all the problems of your life and the world around you that depend on the power of friendship: career success, family relations, a sense of belonging, finding a mission in life and a team to help carry it out, and even bigger issues such as war, poverty, suppression of human rights, and the wasting of the environment. All of these dilemmas ultimately have solutions that rise up from the basic level of how connected we are to each other and the quality of emotion we share in seeking common ground and common goals. Friendships, especially women's friendships, are the glue of society, stronger than any written contract, law, or advertising slogan.

Joni sipped her coffee and stared out the bay window in the kitchen on to the meadow in her backyard. Springtime along the Connecticut River valley was a wonder, a symphony of color, something her artist's eye had never failed to appreciate. Though she'd lived here for three years now, she still found the vision majestic. So utterly different from the Pennsylvania farmland where she grew up and the urban expanse of Greenwich Village where she fulfilled so many of her dreams.

It was beautiful.

And it made her feel horribly lonely.

Craig came down from the bedroom and kissed her on the top of her head. "Thinking about what you're going to paint today?"

She turned to him and saw that he looked as crisp as ever in his Hugo Boss suit. The investment firm he'd started up had enriched him in so many ways beyond sheer financial gain. It had turned him into a pillar of the community, something that gave him extra bounce in his step. He even seriously considered running for mayor. Joni loved him at least as much as she did when she married him, but, like the meadow outside, looking at her professionally attired husband underscored the ever-present sense of emptiness she felt.

Craig turned to pour himself a cup of coffee and Joni got up from her seat.

"Craig, if I don't make a change soon, I'm going to wither up and die."

Craig looked at her nervously, the coffeepot suspended over his cup. "Um, what do you mean, Jo?"

From Craig's expression, Joni could tell that he thought she was starting an entirely different kind of conversation. "This isn't about us," she said with a little chuckle. "I *love* us. It's everything else I'm not so crazy about."

Craig filled his cup and gestured her over to the kitchen table with him. "Really? I thought you loved painting. I thought you loved the house."

"I do. But it's just so quiet sometimes—*most* of the time. And I miss Amy. And Sue. And Tina. And Shauna, Carol, and Kim and everyone else."

"So have them up. Let's set up a weekend a couple of weeks from now when everyone can come. It'll be a huge sleepover party."

Joni smiled at Craig. He'd make a good mayor. "That would be great, and we probably should do it. But then a week later I'll be missing them like crazy again."

"I thought you e-mailed and IM'd those guys regularly."

Joni shrugged. "It's not the same."

Joni stared down at her coffee cup. Birds sang outside, but she couldn't find any sweetness in their song.

Craig reached across the table and placed his hand over hers. "What if we got a pied-à-terre in Manhattan?"

She glanced up quickly. "Really?"

"Yeah. You know I love the city, too. We can go in on weekends and maybe even stick around on Mondays. It would probably even help my business if I spent a little more time schmoozing with people on Wall Street. And when you weren't hanging around with your friends, you could maybe do some more of those fire-escape still lifes I always loved."

"It probably wouldn't help your mayoral ambitions much if you were leaving town every weekend."

Craig shook his head. "I don't need to be mayor, Jo. That was just *a thing*. Let's do this."

"You mean it?"

"I mean it."

Joni's head was spinning. "You know, Tina's a realtor. She could probably find something fantastic for us."

Craig stood up, moved close, and kissed her. "Then you should probably give her a call this morning."

Craig grabbed his briefcase, kissed Joni again, and headed for the door. Joni admired his cute butt for a moment and then went for the phone, feeling vibrantly alive.

What We Can Learn from Carly, Sandra, and Joni

Carly, from the story in the introduction, and Sandra and Joni, the two women you met in this chapter, have "higher brains" that are very different from one another, as the details of their stories make plain. One thing they had in common, though, is that they had negative emotion in their lives. Therefore they had faltering friendships or none at all.

If you delve a bit further into those tales, you'll find the "Shake-spearean" level of drama stored in the mammalian brain. Carly had negative emotion in her life, which further isolated her by driving potential friends away. What's more, the lack of positive emotional energy in her life was compounded by the inconsistent contact she made with potential new friends. From her, we learn that one component of friendship's positive emotional energy is that it must be consistent.

Sandra was a socially talented woman who had a choice to make about a long-tarnished friendship. Her friendship problem centered on being true to her feminine identity, which carries with it a need to be connected to and nurturing of others, yet also to be a self-respecting woman of personal identity separate from her former mentor-gone-bad. Her friendship problem with Tamara was not from a lack of consistency (they were at first consistently positive about each other then consistently negative about each other). Their problem was a lack of mutuality. The relationship of the college days did far more to benefit Tamara (propping her up on a high social horse) than it did for Sandra. Enough experiences of Sandra feeling negative emotion when she was around Tamara temporarily killed the relationship, even though Tamara felt consistently positive emotion about one-upping Sandra. That's another component: the consistent positive emotional energy of friendship must be mutual.

Joni was a woman who had had many great friendships to cherish, most of which would have lasted for decades. Yet, as consistent (and therefore reliable) a friend as she and her friends were to one another, and as mutual as those friendships were, there was something missing for Joni. Something that gnawed at her: there was no opportunity to share feelings on a consistent, mutual basis with other women. The lack of opportunity for sharing not only made her feel malaise in her mammalian brain, it cut right into the lifeblood of feminine instinct in her reptilian brain: the need to belong and share feelings. The consistent, mutual, positive energy of friendship must be shared—ideally, in person.

Through these three stories, we have arrived at a universal definition of friendship, the core of a system for you to analyze every friendship problem you have ever had or ever will have:

Friendship is consistent, mutual, shared positive emotion.

This is the secret code of friendship, the rule and key to diagnosing your problems with friendships and fixing them.

Consistent, *mutual*, *shared*, and *positive emotion* are just four terms, each of which is crucial as a friendship skill. When a friendship is failing, one or more of these four criteria is missing. When a friendship lasts and is durable, happy, and organically blossoming over the years and decades, all four of these are well maintained. The special situation we call "best" friendship arises from an especially complementary matching of personality in terms of the "mutual, shared" part of the definition, which can be cultivated using a technology I developed called KWML™ personality typing (more on that later).

Consistency

When you initially make a friend on the acquaintance level, you may notice that you like her energy. The energy makes you feel good. She's fun, she does interesting things, and she seems to know people. But then you make time for her in your schedule, and maybe she has to cancel. She calls to apologize and reschedules. You meet up eventually and have a great time, just like when you first met, but then a few more weeks go by and she hasn't answered the calls you made to arrange the next time you will meet. Nothing.

Eventually, you start to feel some negative energy about her. It is as if she doesn't respect you, which might not be the case at all (she may have a horrid career schedule). Nonetheless, your budding friendship has gotten off on an inconsistent footing and is unlikely to become a very high-quality friendship later on. You may always think of her as an acquaintance-level friend, but she is not going to be one of your best friends.

Mutuality

You have a new friend who is fun, humorous, and seems connected to other women. You notice how much respect her buddies give her when they are out together. She has routine gatherings where the same people show up to share a sense of belonging.

Yet, over time, you find that the gatherings are always business related and that many of her devoted friends are actually followers that are beholden to her professionally in some way. Knowing her improves their access to clients or to a potential promotion. She takes you a bit under her wing, and you meet in groups regularly but never alone for coffee as you might like once in awhile. Soon, she is asking you to do her a favor here and there. She asks you to call some of the members of the business group to make sure they are coming to the next meeting.

You feel good about this at first because it makes us all feel good to be important to others through helping them. Then she asks you to pick up something for her at the post office on your way to the monthly dinner. You do so without much thought but soon notice that your feelings of friendship with her feel somehow different. You intuit that there's something wrong there.

Finally, she asks you to inform one of the business club members that she doesn't fit in anymore and that she ought not to attend any more meetings. This feels totally unnatural and you stop in your tracks. You ask yourself what your "friend" has ever done to improve your own life. Introduce you to her business friends? Yes, but that is nothing you couldn't have done on your own. You realize there is a problem of mutuality in this relationship and that this woman needs to be knocked down a few pegs on your spectrum of friendship, maybe even back to acquaintance level.

People of very mismatched ability to treat each other with mutual respect and advantage, or even to work as a team that nurtures its femininity, leaves the friendship lacking in both quality and durability. Remember our spectrum:

Spectrum of Friendship Quality

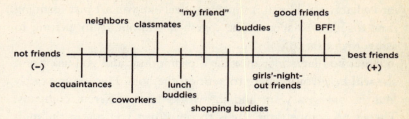

This spectrum parallels the degree of maturity of character and personal growth two people have reached, and to what extent they mutually share in that maturity. We tend to attract friends of a maturity level similar to our own. People are never the same "age" psychologically as they are outside, "biologically."

Sharing

You meet a new friend who is well-known in your city, and your energy is great together. It feels good. She gives you a sense of welcome every time you meet, and you meet consistently. When she makes an appointment, she keeps it. You are in different fields, but your interests and skills complement each other. And there are things you can teach each other.

Now, at first it also feels good to notice how she always splits the lunch tab with you equally and how she seems to enjoy as many of the introductions to your friends as you have to hers. But over the weeks, something feels intuitively wrong. She never seems to want to meet for dinner even though she is always on time for lunch or daytime shopping together. It isn't like she has a husband or children to go home to. She is single and looking, just like you, but you notice that she hasn't shared all that much about her romantic life.

The good feelings fade a little bit at this, and you don't know exactly why. It just feels a little like you're being shut out. She mentions that she had "a rough childhood" but never really goes into what it was like. It is starting to feel like you are just spending time together to spend time together, without really getting to know each other.

Soon you have a chance for a promotion, and you ask her if she will help you prepare to petition the boss. Her job is exactly like the one you want and she works for a different company. There's no competition. Or is there? When you are in the middle of lunch, you ask her exactly how she approached her boss when she first felt ready for the same promotion. Inexplicably, she clams up.

Nothing.

You know that she has real expertise here, but she'll only talk to you about it in vague generalities. This is not the friendship it was originally made out to be. Soon, even though you still meet from time to time, you begin to tell her less and less about your personal life. Your friendship problem is one of lacking sharing ability or desire.

Positive Emotion

You meet a woman who joined your company as recently as you did. You chat and find that you have many hobbies and interests in common. Your husbands even went to the same school. Soon you plan on getting together as couples for dinner, believing your husbands are sure to hit it off. As the weeks pass, you regularly meet but start to share deeper feelings and personal issues. You find that she has been down lately and you are concerned. She tells you she is worried that her husband might leave her soon. You cancel your plans with your husband to make time for her to tell you all about it.

Yet when you meet up you find that she has had a depression problem for years and refuses to get help about it. She tells you how she never seems to be able to hold on to friends and tends to get more and more isolated even as her husband complains that she should "get more of a life" beyond him. When you are done, she says she feels better, but it doesn't really show in her face. She ends the conversation by saying that she always seems to have a friend or two, but none of them last, and maybe you should think deeply about whether you really want to be her friend.

You leave the restaurant with a strange intuition that feels a bit guilty. You think about this and realize you have done nothing wrong. Why should you feel so guilty? You hear from her regularly from then on, about how bad she feels, and a month later you get an emergency call from her that she needs you to come over right away. Her husband has not returned from work even though it is late at night. It turns out that his car broke down, and he arrives home with the driver of the tow truck.

You feel angry and are not sure why. In fact, you feel guilty for even being angry—and this makes you doubly angry. You go home, and for the next few weeks you avoid her calls. It nearly always feels bad to be around her, to talk to her, or to think about her. Your friendship problem with her is the most fundamental of all: there is more negative emotional energy between you than positive energy.

The need we have for positive emotional energy is the absolute core of friendship. If we don't have positive emotions together, we don't have a friendship at all.

Many people share their complaints and negative gossip as their only mode of connection with us. On an intuitive level, though, we don't trust these people very much and don't continue to make time to be with them. Friendship absolutely must be about two people raising each others' emotional energy level into positive, good feelings.

Knowing these four traits of a quality friendship and how they move us along a spectrum of friendship (and maturity) is going to

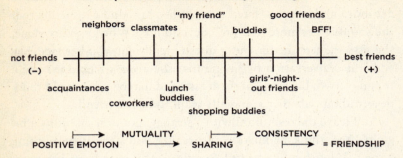

As we move across the spectrum in maturity of character, we increase the quality of our friendships, and we also naturally develop the four master checklist traits of friendship.

This spectrum parallels the degree of maturity of character and personal growth two people have reached, and to what extent they mutually share in that maturity. We tend to attract friends of a maturity level similar to our own. People are never the same "age" psychologically as they are outside, "biologically."

serve you well from here on out. These traits provide a master checklist for diagnosing and fixing (or, on occasion, ending) any friendship problem you have.

What's more, as you learn to master these qualities in many different friendship situations, the number of friends you build will start to propel your life directly, automatically, and scientifically toward success and happiness in life. When you have real tools to deal with friendship problems, they can even become an adventure to enjoy. Everything changes when you know exactly what you are dealing with and what to do next—when you are in on the psychology of friendship.

Throughout this book there will be checklists for you to assess specific aspects of your friendships, but the master checklist for the overall state of your friendships is this:

The Master Friendship Checklist

- Are my friend and I consistent with each other, without large gaps where we don't see each other or during which we treat each other very differently from what we are used to?

- Are my friend and I mutual in how we treat each other, or is it one-sided much of the time?

- Are my friend and I sharing our lives much of the time, in terms of physically being around each other, opening up to how we really feel, and teaming up on activities?

- Are my friend and I feeling positive emotions when we interact far more often than negative emotions (stress)?

Stress and Self-Control of Negative Emotions

In our new definition of friendship as "consistent, mutual, shared positive emotion," we need to start with the "positive emotion" part. The easiest way to identify and fix the worst challenges of friendship is to spot places where we are stressed and to cultivate more control over our own negative emotions.

In my system, I define stress as negative emotional energy coming from outside our *personal boundary*. Your personal boundary distinguishes what you control in life from what you do not. There is much about life we do not control, including the weather, the economy, and certainly other people. Yet ultimately, the things that stress us have origins in other people. Real stresses always arise from negative emotional energy in others. Traffic jams do not put stress on a friendship, even if we are about to meet a friend after just enduring one. We don't have to let the traffic jam have an impact on our emotions. It means us no harm—it just is what it is.

If there is stress in a friendship related to a recent traffic jam, it is caused by our internal emotional reaction to the jam. We project blame onto our friend because we don't have very good boundaries. The jam doesn't carry a negative energy in and of itself. Later I will show you how to handle anger and anxiety that arises from your interpretation of the physical situations around you.

Stress is also not a necessary response to failure, since some people "fail" at reaching their goals and don't get stressed, while others do. And stress is not an inevitable result of being indecisive, since some people are very stressed about being wishy-washy while others feel just fine taking their time to make a major life decision. Stress is only about how we feel, and it is a negative feeling and a negative energy.

If the definition of friendship is "mutual, shared, positive emotion," then as a negative emotion, stress is most certainly a destructive force in friendships. Stress is bad for you, and I don't just mean bad for the cardiovascular and anticancer systems of your body. It dwindles your social network. It needs to be rooted out and eliminated.

If stress is negative energy and negative energy destroys friendships or prevents them from ever getting started, then the first steps in making friends and keeping them are:

- Knowing how to be low stress toward others
- Lessening the stress of others by virtue of your presence

Stress comes in two varieties of negative energy. In my system, you can call these "hurt" and "loss." I have another original equation I discovered for you, and it is the negative parallel of the self-esteem equation, since stress is the emotional opposite of self-esteem:

Stress = Hurt + Loss

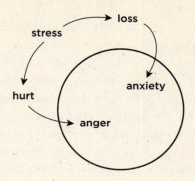

Hurt is a negative energy coming at us from the outside that threatens to do us harm, physically or psychologically. A hurt can be a slight insult, a bee sting, a slap to the face, or a public embarrassment. What is common about all hurts is that if we let them into us, they cause us to feel anger. The stress we call "hurt" is outside of us until we allow it in to become anger. Likewise, an already angry person is far more prone to hurl a hurtful comment at us than one who is not angry in the slightest. If you want to make friends, don't go around being an angry person who hurts the feelings of others all the time.

Loss is also a negative energy stress, the cause of a negative energy emotion called anxiety. Loss comes at us from the outside, too, threatening to deplete our time, energy, health, money, or some other precious psychological resource. If we let loss into us, we feel anxious. A person who takes all of their worries and makes them our responsibility is not likely to become our "best friend forever," as enjoyable as it may be for a short time to complain about life together. If you want to make friends, don't go around being an anxious, worried person who dumps the feelings of loss on others all the time.

A divorce or breakup can carry both hurt and loss, as can being fired, coming down with a major or permanent health problem, moving to a new place, or any of a number of challenges. The point is that you can now divide up what feels like hurt, what feels like loss, and deal with those individual aspects of stress (and therefore friendship woes) efficiently and effectively.

If you examine yourself and get feedback from others about how much stress you cause them versus how much stress you relieve them of, you are well on your way to great skill at making new friends. It really is that simple. Friendship is not necessarily about having the exact same beliefs or goals, the exact same cultural or economic background. It is not about being identical twins. Friendship is the ability to add positive emotion to someone else's life while not adding negative emotion.

Sandra and Tamara had a very rocky start long ago. They shared mutual positive emotion when they were in a sorority together, but it quickly deteriorated into hurting each other, leading to the temporary demise of what could have been a more consistently positive-emotion-based friendship. Tamara hadn't shared with Sandra the fact that her mother was dying and was unwittingly angry at her own mom abandoning her (a feeling many of us would not be aware of or admit to on a conscious level), and this anger and anxiety seeped out into her interactions with Sandra without either of them being consciously aware of it. All the two former friends knew in their hearts was that they felt bad much of the time they were around each other.

A person can bring down friendships in many ways without even realizing it. One of the most common is the absence of the kind of bonding that can be enjoyed simply in sharing. Certainly sharing is one of the four core parts of friendship, but when women frequently share negative things from their lives without sharing positive things, this begins to wear the bonds down. Then you feel a bit guilty about "needing a break" from that friend. To the friend, the avoidance seems inexplicable.

Women who try to make friends when they are in the middle of a major life stress can find themselves in a particularly precarious state. Friendships are so needed during such times, yet carrying the weight of those stresses and losses into a potential new group of friends is a surefire way to sabotage belonging even before the friendships start.

In short, we need to think far ahead in planning the friendship landscape of our lives, so that we have a network that is growing, stable, and available in times of crisis.

We'll begin with a checklist that virtually guarantees that new friendships can easily begin.

The Checklist for Making Friends and Starting Friendships

- Do I carry positive emotion in me today? Do I relieve other people's stress?

- How can I become better at finding positive emotion in me even on short notice, to give away and, through this, provide other people relief from stress?

- Do I generally cause other people to feel hurt, whether I am consciously aware of it or not?

- How can I cause people less hurt and be less angry myself when first meeting people?

- Do I generally cause people to feel loss, worry, or anxiety (theirs or my own) whether I am consciously aware of it or not?

- How can I cause people less of a feeling of loss, less worry about themselves or about me, and be less anxious or worried myself when first meeting people?

- So far, among the people I have met this week, is there anyone with whom I might just pass the master friendship checklist? I will seek more contact with those people.

If there had to be an actual anatomic place in the brain where the core "software" of friendship exists, it would certainly be in the mammalian brain, the center of emotion. We could just stop at the mammalian brain to understand friendship in general. Yet for us to be more than just armchair observers of friendship—and come to a new understanding of how to renovate and amplify our friendships—we will have to learn to "bring our whole brain to the table." We need to examine all three areas of the brain and identify how they influence friendships.

The Three Brains of a Potential Friend

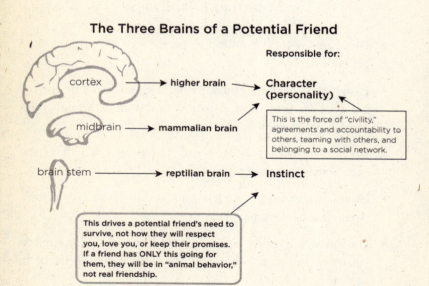

Responsible for:

cortex → higher brain → **Character (personality)**

This is the force of "civility," agreements and accountability to others, teaming with others, and belonging to a social network.

midbrain → **mammalian brain**

brain stem → reptilian brain → **Instinct**

This drives a potential friend's need to survive, not how they will respect you, love you, or keep their promises. If a friend has ONLY this going for them, they will be in "animal behavior," not real friendship.

The reptilian brain is the center of gender-related instincts, the only area of the brain where men and women are profoundly different. If we delve into its mysteries next, we will be well suited to deal with friendship challenges that arise between women and men, as well as understanding how uniquely different men and women are at handling friendship. The next chapter ought to mend some great wounds you have had in the past simply because men and women communicate, love, and navigate friendships differently by instinct. Our gender instincts guide the male or female style with which we seek consistent, mutual, shared positive emotion.

The reptilian brain is the "software" of our instincts. The mammalian brain is the "software" of our emotions and the core of friendship. But the higher brain is the "software" of our character, the brain software that both steers our emotions to good ends through friendship and puts a cap on any naughty doings of the reptilian brain. We need all three to work in synchrony to reach a happy, successful destiny. Let's now survey the landscape of these "three brains" of friendship: the reptilian brain, mammalian brain, and higher brain.

Chapter Two

Feminine and Masculine Instinct: The Reptilian Brain and Friendship

And Pooh said to Piglet, "Life is so much friendlier with two."

—A. A. MILNE

LONG BEFORE the film *When Harry Met Sally*, our culture had more than a twinge of doubt about whether men and women can truly be friends without any sexual overtones. In the movie, Harry might have had a case if he were looking at friendship only as a function of the reptilian brain. After all, it is the behavioral center of human survival and the reproductive instinct, the storehouse of the unconscious, and the only area in the brain where we can clearly say that the core identity of men and women are psychologically *different*.

It is the reptilian brain's evolutionary development that makes us clearly, indisputably feminine or masculine. Friendship is then colored by gender-specific instincts, though it is not completely controlled by them. This means that both men and women have much to learn from each other about friendship, and about the one and only *real* "force" or "energy" that fuels personal success and happiness.

We begin in the reptilian brain because it is the center of all passion—both positive and negative—whether it be romantic passion, passion about a career, passion about life and survival, or passion about friendships. The reptilian brain also makes us want to believe in magic in life and to experience the numinous, the spiritual passion that causes us to trust in something greater than ourselves. It is similar to the older notions of Freud's unconscious, especially the id, or Carl Jung's "shadow" side of our psychology. To theologians it is the home of sin or vice. To the rest of us, if it is blindly determining our behavior, without guidance and mentorship, the reptilian brain is simply immaturity, criminality, or just adolescent, impulsive urges.

If we had only the behaviors driven by the reptilian brain, we would be working exclusively at the level of gender, sexual, and survival instincts, the facts of life we normally learn to deal with in our childhood and adolescence. Maybe that's why older adults sometimes say "kids are such animals" when they see street gang members letting their reptilian brains get the best of them or they hear the cruel things said by "mean girls" who exclude or humiliate their girlfriends at school. It is also why, when those instincts are absent, so very many older adults suffer the pains of social isolation or even a general lack of passion for life.

The reptilian brain is our only source of desire, lust, or passion. We can feel sexual passion about a love affair and survival passion— a passion at the very core of our identity and existence—about a work of art, a career, a child, and certainly a best friend. If there is one aspect of all the survival mechanisms in the reptilian brain that address friendship, it is "strength in numbers," the desperate and passionate need for all men and women *to belong*. To exist in society, we do need to keep the passions of the reptilian brain in check or at least channeled into politically appropriate activity, and yet we also desperately need the passions of our reptilian brain to be manifest—expressed and honored as that which makes us truly masculine or feminine and full of zest for life.

The Importance of Belonging, Connecting, and Communicating

Originally, belonging and communicating were the same for us. There was no e-mail, online dating, cell phones, texting, or even carrier pigeons. Our communication was in person, by spoken word, sight, and touch. When we look at how femininity has an impact on friendship, two ancient stories, the legend of Demeter and Persephone and the legend of Eros and Psyche, come to mind. For how masculinity has an impact on friendship, there is the story of King David and Jonathan, and the story of the Battle of Thermopylae.

Friendship is hardwired in us as a survival skill, especially in the instincts of women. Psychologist Robert Cialdini speaks of what he calls "social proof" in his book *Influence: Science and Practice*. He says, "We view potential actions we take as either correct or desirable to the degree that we see others doing the same actions." Considered perhaps the most powerful force in any marketing campaign, social proof is also a way of expressing the universal human need for survival in our reptilian brains. We tend to buy already popular products as if our very lives depend on it. The instincts of our reptilian brain tell us that if vast numbers of others are using a product, we had better get one, too. To the unconscious mind, our very survival might be at stake, even if we have no logical, conscious reason why.

In the hunter-gatherer cultures we originated from, we could not survive without connections to the rest of our communities. People "like" other people who are similar to them and who appreciate the same things (and therefore buy the same things). If I buy what you buy (books, cars, or clothing, for example), you might like me more because we have something in common. You may then be more likely to protect me or team up with me if I face a crisis or need assistance. I am your friend by virtue of what I buy—what I like. Social proof, then, is just one of the many silent, invisible forces of the human unconscious, which evolved to promote our survival. And belonging is not just a personal preference, a wish, or a desire. It is a hardwired reflex that keeps the race alive.

Portions of the myth of Eros and Psyche directly address the desperate drive in the feminine identity to find belonging through friendship. In the tale, Psyche is the most beautiful mortal female on earth. Due to the jealousy of Aphrodite, the goddess of love and maternity, she is sentenced to marry Death himself. When Aphrodite dispatches her son, Eros, also known as Cupid, to shoot his arrows through her heart, causing her to fall in love with Death, he accidentally pricks himself and wants to make Psyche his wife instead. Through all the twists and turns of marital instinct and growth, Psyche learns how to be both a wife and a feminine woman with her own identity, at one point estranging her god-husband, until she is given impossible tasks to accomplish in order to win him back forever.

During her time in the marital nest, a virtual Garden of Eden, Psyche is not permitted to see her husband's face, as one of his "rules of marriage." She is excited to be married (and not to Death), yet she is dismayed at the lack of intimacy with her husband. At some point, her sisters back in the real world hear of her plight and, jealous of her marital status, plot to have her assert herself, maintaining their power as sisters in her life. When Eros is away, they sneak into the garden and counsel Psyche to take a lamp and a dagger to bed that night. The sisters suggest to Psyche that if her husband will not show her his face, he must surely be a monster of some sort, one who will no doubt eat her one day. They compel her to stab him with the dagger and then light the lamp to see his horrible dead face.

Psyche is conflicted about this advice, of course, as many a woman today would be when advised by close friends to do something "in her best interest" that doesn't feel right. The need to belong to a group of friends is so strong in a woman's reptilian brain that it sometimes causes her to do things that will harm her marriage, career, or even health just for the ongoing permission and identity of belonging.

We can see how this force of femininity might drive many an adolescent girl to drugs in order to belong to a certain crowd. It is at work when a woman is in a dead-end career that makes her miserable, yet she dallies and delays when presented with a chance to change jobs because the office friends are "just so close to me." Nearly every man I have ever met has talked about how his girlfriend wants "to get serious" when her friends start getting married, or how she feels "like I need more space to go out" when her friends become newly single or divorced. The woman's need for belonging is a force that men often do not understand, because it is at the level of passion, a deeply hardwired survival instinct of the reptilian brain.

Ultimately, Psyche grows as a woman when she refuses to follow her sisters blindly. She relies on them only for the call to action in her marriage, the suggestion to look deeper. But the way in which she takes action based on their advice is all her own. She lights the lamp first, *then* pulls out the dagger. As the flickering candle sputters in the darkness of night, she sees that Eros is not a monster. His face is beautiful and he is her husband. All will turn out well. The wax drips on Eros, he awakes, and the marriage moves into further intimacy. Psyche needed her friendly sisters to give her advice and a push, but in the end, her decisions would be hers, and hers alone, to live with.

What of men? What can we learn of their friendships and survival needs to belong? While the reptilian brain gives women a passionate need to belong to a group that shares an identity, men's reptilian brains give them a passionate need to belong to a group that is arranged in hierarchical *rank*, and is on a *quest*. Let's look at the biblical King David and his best friend, Jonathan. Before he was crowned king of Israel, David was a captain in the army of King Saul, a weak and depressive regent who often needed David to sing him songs to lift his spirits. Saul's son, Jonathan, eventually came to be David's dearest and most trusted friend.

As David develops his masculine identity through rising in the ranks of Saul's army, his spirit, drive, and ultimately, friendship ability, are just too much for the weak King Saul to take. Just as Psyche metaphorically aroused the jealousy of Aphrodite through the feminine reptilian-brained instinct to be seen as most beautiful, David aroused the jealousy of Saul through the masculine reptilian-brained instinct to be considered of highest rank among men. Both genders' jealousies arise from comparisons to others in their gender, but for different reasons.

Psycholinguist Deborah Tannen teaches us that the worst thing a little girl can do to another little girl is to *exclude* her from belonging to a group of friends and that the worst thing a little boy can do to another little boy in a group of friends is to publicly one-up him in *rank*. The most effective thing you could do for a male to arouse total reflex allegiance to you would be to assist him in elevating his *rank* among other men. We see this operating in the interventions of Jonathan in the life and rise of David.

When David is reaching his pinnacle of power as one of Saul's loyal servants, he is caught unaware by the first of what will be many assassination plots by the ruler. He is cut and scraped, escaping death. But the far worse wound to David is the instinctual one—that the very man he had faithfully won victories alongside was now trying to kill him. Enter Jonathan, Saul's own son, who sees the errors in his father's character and submits to the force in life that is of an even higher order than official family titles: loyalty to a friend of high character. Jonathan warned David about the very first "death squad" sent by Saul. He saved his best friend's life, even at the risk of angering his own king and father.

David was not, of course, one to fear death. He had been in many a bloody battle and stared death in the eye countless times. What makes men feel a passionate sense of belonging in their friendships is the *assistance* given by other men in protecting and raising their rank among men, not just being allowed to remain in the group. This is the passion triggered in the male reptilian brain. In the case of best friends David and Jonathan, this went to the extent of saving the other's life. What's more, Jonathan saved David's place in history, his legacy to the world as a man.

To be a good friend to other women, in a way that sparks their reptilian-brained passion for your friendship, give them the feeling that they *belong*. To be a good friend to men, in a way that makes them passionately value your friendship, help them achieve high *rank* among men and safety from males who are of higher rank, and show that you support their career strivings, their legacy to future generations.

The Importance of Nurturing Yourself to Be a Good Friend to Others

What of women's legacy to future generations? While women have every right and ability to succeed in a career and find healthy pride in an occupation, they can do something that men can never achieve: they literally give *birth* to the next generation.

A second way that women belong, and therefore feel safe and secure with a passionate sense of identity, is in their connection to their mothers. It is in this very first bonding and connection that women truly learn to nurture *themselves*. Doing so reduces the amount of stress that they put on others in friendship, because it makes them less dependent on others for what amounts to parenting. This kind of belonging and need for motherly nurturing is illustrated well in the myth of Demeter and Persephone.

Persephone, like Psyche, was an immensely beautiful woman, but she was already a goddess. One day, while walking in a field, she was swallowed by the ground as it was torn open by Hades, god of the underworld. Stealing her away to be his wife, Hades enraged Persephone's mother, Demeter. Demeter was so passionately dismayed that she both neglected the maintenance of the earth's formerly flourishing crops and also purposely decimated them in her frantic desire to find her daughter.

Eventually there was an outcry from all of humanity over the famine that resulted, so much so that Zeus struck a deal with Hades. Persephone would return to the world—and her mother—for eight of the twelve months of the year (this is the explanation in Greek mythology for the origin of the seasons. The absence of Persephone's beauty from the surface world is what we all experience as winter).

Women will always instinctually be physically and emotionally closer to their mothers than men are to their fathers. One of a mother's gifts is to reflect our emotions back at us, to teach us what they mean and therefore give us power to use emotions to better our lives. This cannot be done solely by telephone and certainly not by e-mail—it takes a woman's touch to remind you of your femininity in belonging. (Alternatively, one of a father's gifts to us is to push us right out of the home, to train us to swim or sink, to face the elements alone, to drive us toward our independence.)

While the myth of Demeter and Persephone shows how near and dear daughters and mothers are, it also shows that women need a connection to not just what is sisterly about friendship but also what is maturely *maternal* about it. The feminine instinct not only has an impact on female friendships on the individual level of bonding, it is also a lifeline to all that is feminine, nurturing, and maternal—the universal feminine. I have seen many a woman with an otherwise stellar career, fantastic marriage and children, healthy body, and healthy finances, describe feeling painfully, passionately empty, lost, or without identity as a woman. This is usually because she feels disconnected from an exclusively feminine source of universal nurturing—from female friends. This is Persephone in the underworld.

When confronted with the task of growing beyond the instincts of being feminine, into a social community of others, women are charged with finishing the tasks of Psyche and Persephone. Psyche must eventually forsake those in need on her quest to make a true connection to her husband, and Persephone must face life for four months every year without the aid of a connection to the maternal.

When a woman shows her friends not only that she can belong but that she can and will stand on her own if reality demands it, her friendships become stronger and she is capable of richer ones because her friends know that she can fulfill many of her own needs. These women never abandon the need for belonging, but they also never become paralyzed and helpless when life, as it sometimes does, temporarily isolates them.

Men have a different task in connecting to the universal masculine through their friendships. We can see the reptilian instinct connecting men to their identity in the Battle of Thermopylae. It is the story of the most legendary of Spartan battles, a mere 300 warriors against a horde of 250,000 Persian invaders under the command of the god-king Xerxes. Perhaps there has never been a more harrowing, heroic example of pure masculine instinct in friendship than at Thermopylae.

King Leonidas was surprised by a gargantuan army of invaders and sorely lacked any regional assistance to defend against them. He was on his own with only three hundred men at his disposal. What was his decision? To try to negotiate? To call for assistance from neighboring regions and wait for their arrival? No, he had to act, and act now.

The Spartans were a culture of warriors. From the time of boyhood, males were trained to never fear death, to never flee any hardship, to never surrender, and to never retreat, all for the sake of victory. It was a masculine culture in the most reptilian-brained sense—a culture in which belonging and identity were entirely dependent on striving for the goal of victory and status among men of other cultures, leaving a legacy to future generations that rank was more important to preserve than individual lives.

Evolutionary psychology shows us that while males innately behave in ways that promote their ongoing gene lines, this imperative is not always expressed solely through personal survival. Sometimes it requires the protection of their kin at any cost. While every mother would do the same for her individual child, it is a hardwired trait of males, in their friendships, to come together as a group for the physical defense of the group legacy.

In the Battle of Thermopylae, when it came time for the three hundred to be chosen to fight, only men who had already sired children were selected. This stays true to all that is reptilian-brained about masculinity: that once the job of begetting the next generation is done, what is left is the defense of their future. The warriors found a unique power against the enemy through the tradition of interlocking their shields, becoming as one, an impenetrable defense in the strategically clever position of a narrow canyon impasse. Further, they often spoke of hoping for a "good death." They already knew and accepted that they would die one day soon, facing an army of a quarter-million warriors, but they knew instinctively that the ultimate failure of masculinity would not be death. It would be not to share in the identity of men who would do what they could to defend their legacy, their children.

Friendship Is a Matter of Survival

In his landmark book *The Moral Animal*, Robert Wright quotes Charles Darwin on the subject of friendship:

Simply stated, an individual who maximizes his friendships and minimizes his antagonisms will have an evolutionary advantage, and selection should favor those characters that promote the optimization of personal relationships.

This means that both the quality of individual friendships and their total number increase our survivability. In fact, women's overall mental, cardiovascular, and immunologic health has been tied to their degree of social belonging and connection. In December 2006, Ed Edelson of HealthDay reported on a new study about the direct health benefits of women's friendships:

Women who sleep well and have good friends have low blood levels of a rather nasty molecule called interleukin-6, a new study finds.

That's important because elevated levels of IL-6 have been linked to diseases ranging from Alzheimer's disease to rheumatoid arthritis to cancer, said study author Elliot M. Friedman, a University of Wisconsin psychologist. . . .

Friedman said he's been studying "what kind of psychological processes seem to be able to influence biological markers that are linked to disease." But while studies by other researchers have looked at negative indicators, such as stress or depression, he has been looking at positive indicators (such as friendship).

So, just as research in the past several decades has shown the impact of depression and anxiety on physical health, we are starting to see evidence of the effect of quality (or lack of) friendships on physical health as well. This makes great sense in my model, for we are defining friendship as "shared positive emotion" (shared self-esteem), and we can directly trace a chronic lack of self-esteem as correlating with depressive and anxiety conditions.

What's more, women can apply the Darwinian view of "survival" to romantic and childbearing survival, career survival, and financial survival. Friends in high numbers and of high quality clearly help us "survive."

We have learned that to increase the total number of friendships you have with women, you need to cultivate an expanding network for yourself that instinctively causes other women to feel welcome and gives them a sense of belonging and nurturing.

Let us end our exploration of the reptilian brain and friendship with a checklist for passion in friendship—without, of course, forgetting the master checklist from the previous chapter.

The Checklist for Passion in Friendship

- If my friend is a woman, do I offer her welcoming, a sense of belonging?

- Does she offer welcome and belonging to me?

- Do I offer some nurturing, some level of maternal guidance and communication when she is in a time of trouble, stress, or disconnection?

- Does she do the same for me?

- Do I respect her need to be passionately feminine, to seek nurturing belonging to a group of women who simply enjoy connecting? Do I help her feel safe and secure? And when she is in a time of personal winter, do I encourage her independence and ability to solve her own problems, her ability to make it to springtime?

- If my friend is a man, do I offer him assistance in raising his rank among other men?

- Does he do the same for me?

- Do I help him achieve greater independence and self-reliance?

- Does he encourage me through example, assistance, and teamwork at being even more independent and self-reliant?

- Do I respect his need to be passionately masculine, to seek higher status or rank, and to belong to a "band of brothers"?

Chapter Three

The Secret Psychology of Groups: The Higher Brain and Friendship

One loyal friend is worth ten thousand relatives.
—EURIPIDES

"YOU CAN'T choose your family, but you can choose your friends," they say. Nowhere is this more relevant than to the higher brain, where we can make logical choices and bring wisdom to the mammalian brain's custody of friendship. One story actually ties this higher-brain concept to the feminine instinct of the reptilian brain. It can help you visualize how we may use all three "brains" in friendship to convey our character—thereby changing the destiny of our future happiness and success.

Hestia is the ancient Greek goddess of home, hearth, and friendship. She is an example to us of how friendship is founded by creating harmony by providing for the comfort of many. Hestia was an exemplar of feminine beauty and grace, features that caught the attention of male gods from Poseidon to Apollo to Priapus, the erect male god of masculine lust. They all competed intensely for her, though their intentions ranged from marriage to the ancient Olympian equivalent of a one-night stand.

But Hestia would have none of it. She said that the ways of Aphrodite (goddess of romance and marriage) were not her ways. She placed her hand on Zeus and swore an oath that she would never marry. More than anything, she wanted to follow a path that was of her own choosing. She didn't fit into the role of a goddess of dominant power or adventure (like Athena, Artemis, or other virgin, unmarried goddesses). She was, though, perfectly content and fulfilled being simply of service to her family and community.

Zeus was grateful for Hestia's willingness to avert the risk of war between her rival suitors and not only supported her wish to remain single but announced that Hestia's name would henceforth be mentioned first in any prayer, that she would be honored with the first sacrifice, and that she would be honored in the temples of each of the Olympian deities.

This myth underscores the deep importance of friendship in society. None of the other gods can operate in world affairs without the peaceful role of Hestia, the goddess of friendship. For women of today who choose to remain single and determined in their individual contribution to the community, here is ancient, hidden support of your foundational role in all society.

Friendship does not require passion or romantic love. Nor does it require high station, leadership, partnership, rules, regulations, or responsibility other than that of giving to others. It only requires Hestia's consistent tendency to support others, love them (which is giving them positive emotional energy), and value their comfort.

Zeus was so delighted with Hestia's decision that he gave her unrestricted access to Mount Olympus, granted her a position as its manager, and granted her the responsibility of running that vast estate while the rest of the gods and goddesses wandered the larger world. True to her nature, Hestia stayed home, never leaving Mount Olympus, always there to welcome others home. She never involved herself in the fights and manipulations of the other gods and goddesses, somehow managing to stay above the fray. Nonjudgmental and forgiving, her unconditional love and calm acceptance inspired the love and trust of others in return. Dependable and caring, Hestia was always there for them and helped them manage their own exciting lives.

You might notice that Hestia's actions were distinctly feminine in terms of reptilian-brain instinct. She valued making a home and securing it and making it comfortable, just as the primordial hunter-gatherer females did. Beyond that, though, her role and example to us is one of actually stabilizing conflict and making peace among all of humanity.

These additional traits of friendship rise high above the level of animals belonging in herds, or even above the core nature of friendship being that of spreading love, but to the level that only the human higher brain provides: harmony among groups and the building of a civilized society. These are friendship traits of high maturity, win-win thinking, wisdom, and exemplary personal-boundary skills.

In other words, Hestia had good boundaries. One of her most important responsibilities to Zeus and all the Olympians was to be "keeper of the reserves," seeing to it that all her clothing and equipment were in good repair and that the pantry was always full so there would be ample ambrosia and nectar on hand when any of the gods or goddesses returned from their adventures. As keeper of all the supplies, Hestia managed the large household, pleasing all with her practical dependability. Our sense of personal boundaries is responsible for all the budgeting ability we possess—putting time, energy, money, and all other psychological "resources" in their perfect place to cultivate our lives, just as Hestia did with the physical resources of Mount Olympus.

If we look to the ancient symbolism used in cults of Hestia devotees, we find the circle, representing the goddess as integrated, a "whole goddess," complete in her feminine maturity, and complete as a being in general. She was seen as not only psychologically centered but as the center of home and family, the city, and even the world itself. The Olympic torch originally honored Hestia—Hestia's fire has been passed through the ages of ongoing civilization.

Just as the symbol of the circle represented Hestia's role in psychological and social integration, we are going to find a direct and practical use for the circle in our own foray into the psychology of friendship. The circle represents twin properties of maturity in our mammalian brain and higher brain: the concept of psychological integration (from the KWML model of four personality types I have identified in my professional work—test yourself at www.kwml.com) and the central power of budgeting our resources, respecting self and others, their rights and responsibilities, and a place of honor among all others who know us: the personal boundary.

The reptilian brain is not exactly discriminating as to *whom* we befriend. It runs on instinct, the illogical, passionate desire in women to *belong* to a group of friends (sometimes without regard for the quality of that group), and the illogical, passionate desire in men to lead or achieve rank in a group of friends (once again, sometimes without regard for the quality of that group).

Consider a fortyish woman who has lost her husband of twenty years to cancer suddenly finding solace in the partying life of a group of late-twentyish neighbors. They accept her. She doesn't know why, but she just feels good and safe among them. To all her former married friends, she is an enigma, but the switchback in her life trail nonetheless temporarily improves her mental and physical health. It doesn't need to be logical. It is instinctive reflex.

In any true quantum approach to psychology, we need to learn first what the outer reaches of each end of a spectrum of behavior are. In terms of friendship, the reptilian brain is the most impersonal and "me-centered" aspect. It is the level of acquaintance, friendships of convenience, and general human companionship.

On the other end of the friendship spectrum would be friendships of the highest and most mature order. These would be "best" friendships, committed friendships, or partnerships that entail duty, responsibility, respect, honor, rules, and promises kept. This level of friendship involves one's word being worth gold. It is only at this level of friendship that one can exist in a stable place within a group and capture the full value from and contribution to *networks* of friends.

Being "Cool" and Using Your "Cool Eye"

Many of us feel as if we are passengers on a bus called fate. We may have had letdowns in life (like Carly in the introduction), failed friendships or romantic attachments, job setbacks, you name it. Over time, bad habits can take root, among the worst being the habit of *passiveness*. Some of us can get so passive about the social connections around us, we can even start to blame all of our failures on the very people *we* let down. In the end, just like Hestia, we will have to be the ones to take action to correct our social connections. If we want to change the world around us, we will literally have to change ourselves. The very first step toward this is cultivating your *Cool Eye*.

We can actually define and measure scientifically such a common pop-culture notion as "being cool." Those who are "cool" appeal to a broad range of people. The most significant reason for this is that they observe themselves enough to avoid flying off the handle, saying inappropriate or offensive things, or taking actions impulsively that cross other people's limits. Having this self-observation ability, the Cool Eye, gives you the ability to "read" the condition, needs, desires, and personality style of *others* at the same time as you read your own. It is a bridge between "me" and "other" that can bring them together in harmony, expand the quality of your friendships, and even help you manage multiple friendships at the same time by "seeing the social landscape" before making your moves within it.

People who don't realize they have a dusty old Cool Eye sitting in their higher brain just don't get it. They are those of us who hours, days, or even weeks after a social interaction, smack their foreheads and say, "What was I thinking? Why did I say that?" or "Why didn't I do something different?" The primary reason we have social regrets is that friendship mistakes come when we do not have our Cool Eyes turned on.

The Cool Eye is your ability to step outside yourself, look at the social situation, observe, and then advise yourself about the best thing to do. It is like being your own social coach, your own wise parent, and your own psychiatrist. There are several ways to access this skill.

First, let's look at where your mind is in terms of *time*. We regard time in one of three ways: the past, the present, and the future. We all know people who are difficult to connect with because they are always thinking about the past. They might be pleasantly reminiscing or they may be reviewing a grudge they have against us, but one thing is certain: they are not in the present with us. Some other people we know are always distracted and hard to connect with because they are too focused on the future. They might be dreamers who are thinking of the next big idea they want to bring up in conversation or are distracted with their urgent plans to get to the next party that night. Again, they don't connect with us here and now. When we, or people we know, are in the past or future in our heads, we are not freely available to connect with others. In general, this is not considered "cool." We might even say someone like this is "on autopilot" or acts like a robot instead of "being real."

Part of what makes a friendship feel truly alive comes from the definition that biologists use for describing all living things. They

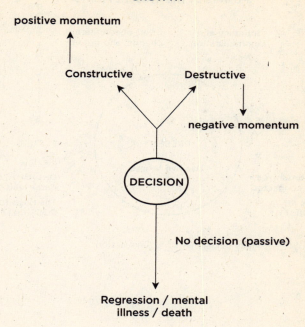

GROWTH

positive momentum

Constructive   Destructive

negative momentum

DECISION

No decision (passive)

Regression / mental
illness / death

say, "Life is irritable." That does not mean a living thing is in a bad mood all the time. It means that the environment does things to a living thing, and the living thing does things back. Being alive, then, is defined by *making decisions.*

All the decisions we make in a friendship are either *constructive*, win-win—benefiting us and our friend—or else they are *destructive*, lopsided, win-lose decisions. Using the definition from biologists, then, the most "alive" friendships are ones where we are *active*, deciding things together *on purpose*. This is why some friendships feel stale, regress, or die. They are not alive in a biological sense because one or the other person is being too passive

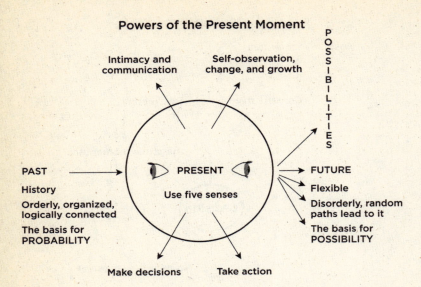

Powers of the Present Moment

in them, lacking a sense of purpose for being together. Any action or decision in your friendship is better than none at all, because you can always use your Cool Eye to learn from mistakes and adjust the course of your friendship. Interestingly, we can only be active and make decisions when we are living in the present.

Your Cool Eye only works when you are *present-minded*. You can encourage present-mindedness through meditation and prayer, writing in a journal, and even yoga. These activities, and the Cool Eye skills that comes from them, place us squarely in the driver's seat in our lives. We can actually observe ourselves before saying or doing things and observe others' needs, desires, and personality styles *at the same time*.

The second thing you can do to cultivate your Cool Eye is to maintain intimate connection with others. When, rather than going off into some reverie about the past or worry about the future, you put your attention on others, you both make a true connection and stay in the present.

A third way is to notice how your senses work. We cannot taste something from the future, smell something from the past, or hear something from either. It is only in the present that our senses work. Yes, we can have memories of sights, smells, or sounds, and fantasies about touches or tastes, but they are never as vivid and immediate as they are in the present. Remembering that you have five senses, then using them purposefully, can also cultivate your Cool Eye. With it, you will rarely have regrets in your social life.

We all have heard of having a "sixth sense," intuition or gut feeling about the future, especially with regard to our social interactions. Many people who've sought counseling with me have had experiences where they went on a second, third, or fourth date with someone who turned out to be very wrong for them or took a job they just "had a bad feeling" about and then were miserable or fired a few months later. Part of what you will learn via my system for analyzing friendship is what I call a Seventh Sense™. This is something beyond just a gut feeling about socializing. Instead, it is both a sense of *where* others are coming from and *why*. Using your Cool Eye is the first step to this ability.

Looking at two other things that can only be done in the present—making a *decision* and taking an *action*—gives us two more activities that cultivate Cool Eye ability. We can't make decisions or take action in the past; it is gone. We also can't make decisions or take action in the future; it isn't here yet. Simply daring to try some social behaviors you aren't used to in your friendships will give you new self-observation ability. If you have trouble saying no to friends, then disagreeing with others, as a learning experience, will help you grow more "cool." If you have trouble telling others about your feelings, then try doing so and learn from the experience. Do not be afraid.

Ways We Spend Time

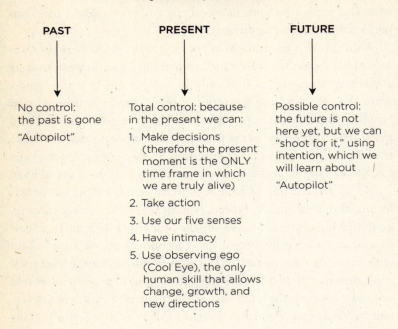

PAST	PRESENT	FUTURE
No control: the past is gone	Total control: because in the present we can:	Possible control: the future is not here yet, but we can "shoot for it," using intention, which we will learn about
"Autopilot"	1. Make decisions (therefore the present moment is the ONLY time frame in which we are truly alive)	"Autopilot"
	2. Take action	
	3. Use our five senses	
	4. Have intimacy	
	5. Use observing ego (Cool Eye), the only human skill that allows change, growth, and new directions	

Our philosopher-adviser Epictetus, who gave us the foundational principle for elevating the qualities of our friendships—"Character is destiny"—also once said, "If you want to improve, be content to be thought of as foolish and stupid." If you are willing to look like a fool for the sake of growing, you will eventually find you can master coolness in friendship.

You might even combine the activities above to exercise your Cool Eye at a shared meal. Many business experts cite the value of "breaking bread" as a way of encouraging friendship with clients and partners, and dining with others uses all five senses to accomplish intimate connection. It is perhaps one of the most present-minded activities we engage in.

Many of you need to drive to get to work. Most of you probably don't even notice the drive anymore. Where was your mind during the trip? Chances are it was in the past or the future—reviewing what yesterday was like or planning your vacation for next week. You weren't in the present during the drive, and, in effect you were on *autopilot*.

Autopilot impairs our ability to cultivate friendships because when we are on autopilot, the world around us gives us only what is convenient for it. In effect, it dumps its leftovers on us. Without your Cool Eye, you get the leftovers of life: the job no one else wanted, the friends no one else wanted, and ultimately the life no one else wanted. To turn this around, exercise your Cool Eye and be at the steering wheel of life.

There are, then, the following general Cool Eye exercises:

- Imagine stepping outside your body to look on the social situation you are in, and advise yourself of the right thing to do next
- Do present-minded activities like writing in a journal, meditation, and yoga
- Focus on other people and their needs and desires: establish intimacy
- Take action, like trying on new behaviors in your friendships
- Make decisions, like scheduling meals with some new friends
- Use your five senses (and eventually a sixth and seventh)

Practice using your Cool Eye in public by stopping to ask yourself internal questions as people socialize with you. *Why is she saying that? What is he probably going to do next? What do these people need in order for them to accept me with open arms?* Your Cool Eye will become your best friend and adviser. Over time, you will have used science to build up your ability to be cool.

The Wonders of Your Personal Boundary

In your friendships, did you ever feel "dissed," disrespected, violated, betrayed, lied to, walked on, overloaded, frazzled, too leaned on, as if your plate was too full, stressed, intimidated, manipulated, accused of being in denial, that you've been used, abused, gossiped about, messed with, experienced "high drama," or any of a host of other unpleasant experiences?

Would you believe that these and hundreds of others are *all* caused by just *one* skill lacking in our lives and those of our friends? That's right, it's the *personal boundary*.

One of the benefits of using a quantum model of psychology is that it helps us simplify and economize on our learning. If I show you just this one single skill, it will help you solve literally hundreds of difficult friendship problems with the very same knowledge and practice.

Your personal boundary is one of the most mysterious things about understanding psychology. It is utterly invisible, yet very real—so real in fact that at times, your very life may depend on its being operational. However, finding and strengthening your personal boundary goes directly against the normal, natural feminine instinct to be connected to others. (Many women feel guilty about using personal boundaries because of this.) The boundary gives you the ability to say no to others—to *exclude* others who are not behaving in a way that works for you right now.

Solid boundaries are always a good thing. They indicate to friends that you are mature (and therefore qualify as a potential best friend), that you are self-respecting, respect others, and can be trusted with even the most sensitive of secrets. This is more than a fair trade-off for occasionally having to say no to others.

Have you ever crossed the border of a country? Did you happen to look at the ground as you crossed? Was there a painted, dotted line going off to the horizon? No, of course not. Yet what would happen if you were to try to cross the border without a passport? Hopefully, you would be stopped. So even though the border of a country is invisible to the eye, it is nonetheless real. The very same thing is true of your personal boundary.

Your boundary marks territory for you. Both physical and psychological territory are inside it, including all things you might consider private and intimate. Your rights are in it, your preferences, beliefs, values, emotions. Personal information like your life's history, experiences, stories you have to tell, and even your freedom of choice are inside it as well. It marks all that you currently *control* about life, from all that you do not.

The American Declaration of Independence states that "All (people) are created equal . . . endowed with unalienable rights . . . among these are life, liberty, and the pursuit of happiness . . ." One question I ask at nearly every seminar I conduct is, "What is *unalienable*?" In describing human rights, the founders were referring to an inherent quality that "cannot be taken away." Not by a stranger, not by a family member, not by a friend, not by a boss, not even by a powerful government. The sense of human rights is a principle of respect and recognition of the personal boundary of even the poorest, least-known, most remote, and unconnected person on earth.

The personal boundary is one of the most important things you will ever learn about in your lifetime. It defines you, protects you. Becoming acquainted with its use will largely determine your destiny through the quality it brings to your friendships. Think of it as an invisible circle drawn around your feet, one that marks all that belongs to you psychologically as well as physically. This circle distinguishes what you control in life from what you don't. It is so strong that even if the most powerful person, company, or government in the world wanted to tell you what to say, feel, or think, they could not penetrate the power of your personal boundary.

The author and psychoanalyst Viktor Frankl wrote about the experience of being in a Nazi concentration camp during World War II. He studied why some people survived and some didn't, even when the wretched, extremely stressful conditions under which the victims lived were the same. What he found was that those who had a reason to live (in his case, to be able to warn his grandchildren of the atrocities he had witnessed), generally did. Those who did not, perished. Even in the most restrictive, physically controlled environment one could imagine—a Nazi concentration camp—there was a force in the survivors that even a brutal enemy could not penetrate. It was the personal boundary.

Even when you think you are "stuck" in your life or in your social situation, you can never truly be. Your ultimate freedom, your power to get unstuck, is contained in the unalienable choices made within your personal boundary.

The founders mention unalienable rights to "life, liberty, and the pursuit of happiness." Our lives form a narrative of our *thoughts*, or intellect. Liberty is the same as freedom of *decision*. And the pursuit of happiness is the same as the process of cultivating positive *emotion* in our lives—friendship. These are the three general features of the human psyche found within the personal boundary, and which I include in my model of the mind.

We control and possess everything inside the boundary. In friendships of lower quality (lacking higher-brain maturity), a friend may tell you how to feel, what to think, what is right and wrong, without even consulting you. In other words, they take over *your* right to make your own decisions. But in mature friend-

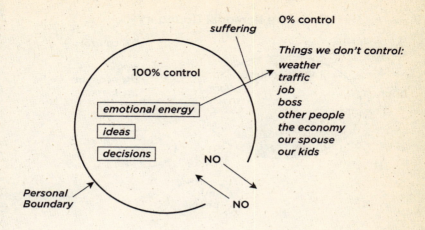

ships of higher quality, the friend actually respects your opinions, respects your feelings, and respects your decisions as yours and yours alone, and they can be supportive of whatever you choose for yourself. The personal boundary is responsible for this aspect of friendship quality.

Immature boundaries are the cause of all the suffering we experience. To borrow from Buddhist doctrines and definitions, suffering is "trying or wishing to control the uncontrollable." When I am stuck in rush-hour traffic, I often clench my fists and wish it would move more quickly. My blood pressure rises and I might even curse. I am, in essence, *wishing I controlled the uncontrollable*. I am *suffering*. Doing this costs me a tremendous amount of energy, energy I could put to good use in cultivating my friendships. This is an immature use of boundaries. The proper response to the uncontrollable rush-hour traffic is to turn on my Cool Eye to assess what I *do* control about rush hour. What resources do I have inside my boundary to bring to bear on the problem? Well, I

The Personal Boundary

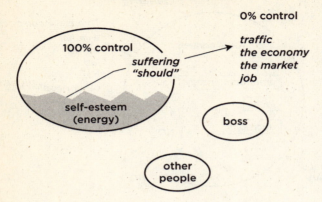

can make a *decision* to turn off at the next exit and use my bright ideas and *intellect* to find another route home. I can enjoy music on the radio, plan my evening, or even use a headset to make phone calls to friends or family (using the time to fill up on good energy and hopefully give some out as well).

Personal boundaries can have gaps, flaws, or what I call *boundary holes* in them. A boundary with a large number of holes is an *immature boundary*. People who do not use their Cool Eye are full of excuses for why the world is so cold and cruel to them. We, of course, do not think they are very good friends. Detecting a large number of holes in a person's boundary immediately tells you that there is a future likelihood of her:

- Being irritable and angry at you over trifling things
- Lying to you, often at the worst possible moment
- Gossiping about you to the worst possible people who can do you the most damage

- Leaning so heavily on you for support that it saps your energy and may even affect your physical health
- Invading your privacy, often to ends embarrassing to you
- Interfering with relationships of yours, endangering or changing them forever
- Heavily draining your resources of time, energy, reputation, and money
- Traumatizing, abusing, or at least "using" you
- Acting "entitled" or in prima donna–like fashion

We suffer only in places in our boundary where there are holes. Perhaps the word we use most often when we suffer is *should*. This word can be an automatic indicator to us that a friend has holes in her boundary. When a friend or potential friend frequently says things like "traffic should move faster," "the weather should be warmer by now," "this city should have lower taxes," or "my boss should give me a raise," that person is a *habitual sufferer*. She has quite a few holes in her boundary, and she works hard to make sure those holes stay wide open. When you get closer to that person, she might start saying: "You really *should* treat me with more respect." "You should meet me every Thursday for a girls' night out." "You should get a different hair style, more like mine. You should go to my hairdresser." Or anything of the like. It gets worse. The next wave is: "You should lend me the money I need this month, and if you don't, you're mean." Or, "You really should make me your new business partner, and if you don't, you're stupid," and other demands of that ilk.

Having holes in our boundaries can parallel all the other childish traits (entitlement; selfishness; impulsiveness or impatience; unwillingness to cooperate, compromise, or work as a team; guilt-tripping; "poor me" attitude; manipulativeness; and jealous competitiveness). Most of us say the word *should* once or twice a week or even a day.

"Thin Skin": Holes in the Boundary

STRESS

STRESS

100% in our control

ME
("overwhelmed")

STRESS

0% in our control

my boundary

This in itself doesn't mean we're childish or have immature boundaries, but I am giving you extreme examples as a tool.

A *thin-skinned* person is someone who is psychologically weak, lacking in fortitude against the stresses of life. When you learn to use the diagrams of my system, you can literally start to see the processes going on psychologically in your friendships. You develop more than just intuition about people—you know why you are having that intuition because you can see the science behind it. It is a "seventh sense" of people. Our Seventh Sense then tells us that people with thin-skinned boundaries lack maturity. With this diagram, you can see why they are immature and why we feel the way we do around them.

We discussed at the beginning how one of the most threatening forces to any friendship is that of stress. It turns out that the mature personal boundary skills that our higher brain helps us achieve establish a boundary surface that has no (or few) holes in it. It is a solid boundary and it resists stress well. People with mature boundaries that lack holes have great *personal strength*.

The boundary also gives shape to our *identity*, the sum total of what makes us unique individuals. The boundary lets us set pref-

Effects of Boundary Holes

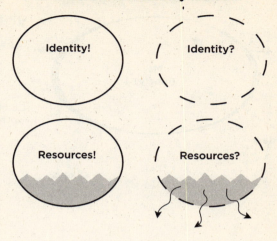

erences in life and therefore distinguishes from others by virtue of those preferences. As a result, if the shape of our boundary is a dotted line full of holes, it is hard to recognize what we really stand for. However, if it is the shape of a solid circle, people can clearly see who we are, what we stand for, and whether they might have a great deal in common with us. Through preferences, the boundary lets us decide between what we tend to say yes to in life versus what we say no to. It also acts like a container to hold and protect our valuable resources.

If I tell you that I generally say yes to dogs and no to cats, that tells you something about my identity as a potential friend. If I go on to tell you that I say yes to rock music and no to country music, and yes to pizza and absolutely no to eggs, then doesn't that say quite a bit about my identity as a person, if only in three nearly trivial areas of life? Imagine how well you would know a friend if you were familiar with dozens or even hundreds of their preferences.

"Thick Skin": Walls in the Boundary

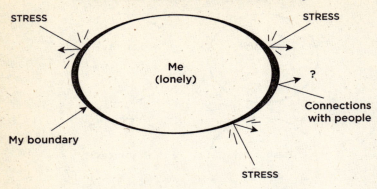

Sometimes people are very closed off and don't easily reveal who they are or what they prefer. These folks have developed what you might call "walls" in the boundary. These are places of psychological scar tissue from being hurt or invaded too much in youth. No amount of energy expended to get them to open up will work. They are going to permanently say no to talking about certain issues.

The friend with walls in her boundary can appear to be very tough and resistant to stress, but this is not the same as mature strength of boundaries. The walls say no to every request for intimacy or sharing, one of the four prime features of friendship in your master checklist. What's more, the walls leave the friend lonely and "starving" for emotional connection, much as a country with locked borders becomes isolated from the international community.

The hole-in-the-boundary effect occurs in three forms: *perfectionism*, *projection*, and *dishonesty*.

When we are perfectionist in our friendships, we see distant goals outside our boundary as if we "should" already have achieved

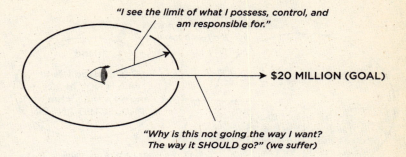

Perfectionism = Not seeing our limits, and feeling as if we "should" already possess goals we have not yet reached

"I see the limit of what I possess, control, and am responsible for."

$20 MILLION (GOAL)

"Why is this not going the way I want? The way it SHOULD go?" (we suffer)

them. One example of this is a man who was very down on himself because his friends had all achieved $20 million in real estate holdings and, at age twenty-eight, he had only achieved $1 million in worth. This tweaked his male reptilian brain in terms of feeling lower in rank because he looked out that hole at their goals instead of seeing his own.

Projection happens when we unwittingly use our boundary holes to eject all the "bad" in us onto other friends and keep only a self-image that is positive, and makes us feel good inside. We all have some good and some bad in us, some positive opinions about ourselves ("I like my hair") and some negative ones ("I make a fool of myself sometimes"). As children, this was a useful strategy for feeling good and even making friends (because displaying positive emotion is the very core of friendship), but this is done at great cost to some friendships, even while temporarily benefiting others.

Sooner or later, the friends who manage to remain in our favor will spot us doing this to others and feel a bit put off or in danger themselves of being demonized. Projection is the very same process that occurs in every corporation in the world when an employee is

Projection = Taking the bad in us and accusing a friend of having the bad quality so we feel better about ourselves. The cause of scapegoating, gossip, and slander

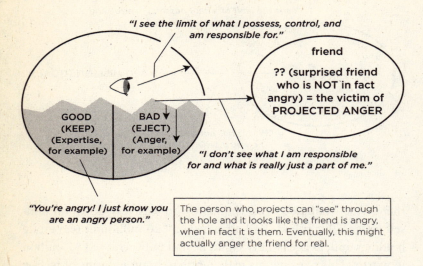

"I see the limit of what I possess, control, and am responsible for."

friend

?? (surprised friend who is NOT in fact angry) = the victim of PROJECTED ANGER

GOOD (KEEP) (Expertise, for example)

BAD (EJECT) (Anger, for example)

"I don't see what I am responsible for and what is really just a part of me."

"You're angry! I just know you are an angry person."

The person who projects can "see" through the hole and it looks like the friend is angry, when in fact it is them. Eventually, this might actually anger the friend for real.

scapegoated, and when friends gossip hurtfully about members of their group.

When we are dishonest with our friends, or they lie to us, it is also caused by holes in our boundaries. A lie can be a manipulation, in some cases an unethical intent to deceive, but in other cases the liars may even have convinced themselves that what they are saying is true. Many times in our friendships, especially when there is codependence, we feel fearful that the truth may hurt our friend or hurt us. A lie is in that case influenced by thinking that we owe the other person something we don't want to give (like a private bit of info) and works much like a smokescreen over the hole in our boundary where we let ourselves feel pressured by the friend to reveal something.

Lies and Boundary Holes

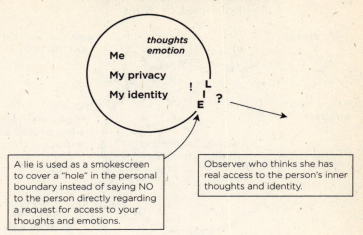

A lie is used as a smokescreen to cover a "hole" in the personal boundary instead of saying NO to the person directly regarding a request for access to your thoughts and emotions.

Observer who thinks she has real access to the person's inner thoughts and identity.

The lie relieves the self-imposed pressure from the friend, yet keeps the codependent appearance that we are revealing all our inner thoughts or feelings. In this way, the lying friends both keep their privacy but also fraudulently maintain the benefits of a quality friendship, which often demands at least some degree of shared intimacy—remember our master checklist.

While both holes and walls in a boundary are considered immature and do not benefit us in higher quality friendships, there is a third kind of quality to the boundary that does make us mature friends. This is having a *door* in your boundary and encouraging friends to have them as well. Doors allow us to be discriminating and to open and close ourselves to intimacy depending on our personal preferences and the current behavior of our friends.

You might notice that in this situation, people have the ability to work their doors according to what is healthy versus unhealthy for them in friendship. None of us is perfect. We all have our bad

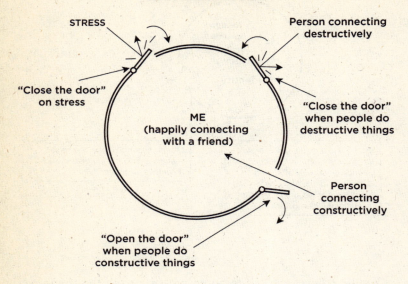

A Mature Boundary with Doors, not Holes or Walls

STRESS

Person connecting
destructively

"Close the door"
on stress

ME
(happily connecting
with a friend)

"Close the door"
when people do
destructive things

Person
connecting
constructively

"Open the door"
when people do
constructive things

days and can't be perfect friends all the time. We say and do things that are off-putting to others at times, but this doesn't have to be the end of the world. All we need to do to have mature relationships is to use good judgment at all times as far as what we agree to ("Yes, I'll go out to eat with you tonight because I have the time and enjoy your company") versus what is bad for us or doesn't suit our preferences ("No, I will not do pot just because you think it's okay").

We can stop suffering by patching the holes in our boundaries— by getting proficient at using the word *no* and hearing the word with grace and acceptance.

We can even do something more than patching holes in our friendships. We can actually replace suffering by doing the *opposite*, which is using *intention*.

Intention

An easy way of envisioning intention comes from the saying teachers tell students in grade school, "It's better to shoot for the stars and land in the mud than to shoot for the mud and make it." What this tells even the youngest student is that if we aim high, we'll likely miss our goals at first, but with some adjustment we will be a whole lot closer to success than if we focused on the negative (or things we can't control, to be more accurate).

If we see intention as focusing on a goal with positive energy, maintaining good self-esteem, and persisting in finding ways around obstacles with creativity until we approach the goal—"shooting for the stars" if you will—we learn from each attempt. In visual form with the elements of our character intact, we get a clear picture of what it is to realize a successful destiny:

Boundaries, Suffering, and Intention

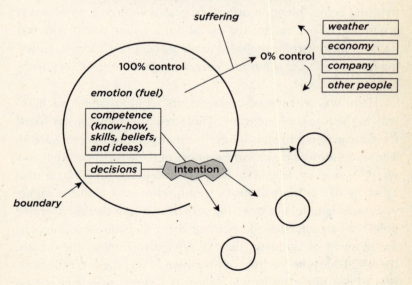

In the diagram comparing suffering and intention, we can clearly see the childhood saying about shooting for the stars versus the mud. Suffering is where we burn one of the resources of our character—emotional energy—on silly things we don't control. With intention, we instead accept for now what we don't control (good boundaries), but we use our intellectual abilities, our education and experience, to:

- Plan for where and when we can take the opportunity to move toward a goal
- Be creative about getting around obstacles in our way

If our Cool Eye is turned on, we see opportunities when they arise, and it is then that we commit our energy to a sure thing. We decide. Remember, making decisions is the biologists' definition of life, so we are "really living" when we use this form of intention. We guarantee an advance toward our goals, and therefore success, by using active intention instead of passive suffering. Intention is a wise use of our energy, the use of our intellect paired with our decision making to be prepared to place energy into action. Suffering is not. Suffering is burning energy on the uncontrollable, without purpose.

There was a study of car accidents along a stretch of highway in the Kansas wintertime. This stretch was known for black ice, a dangerous and invisible peril to many an unsuspecting driver. The study showed that a large number of the wrecks ended in cars wrapped around telephone poles. These were, however, spread apart by half a football field's length. How was it that a highly unexpected number of surviving casualties would hit the telephone poles? When interviewed, many of them said the same thing: at the moment of skidding, they all tended to look at the danger, the telephone pole (because our reptilian brain takes over the function of our other brains when there is a threat to our lives, and

The Personal Boundary and Suffering

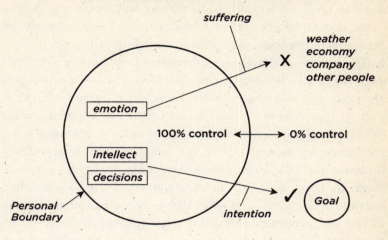

we need it to do so to protect ourselves from danger). However, in this case, the old reptilian brain lets us down. By focusing on the telephone poles while in the hands of a technology our ancient brains could not have anticipated—steering wheels—the drivers actually steered *into* the poles! This is suffering, and only good practice with your Cool Eye can prevent your reptilian brain from taking over the rest of your brain at the most inconvenient times.

Friends of a Feather Flock Together

Having doors in your boundary allows you to be a great budgeter of your resources, to use them in just the right way to build even more, to increase your total number of friendships and their quality, to protect yourself from stress, drama, and manipulation without eliminating all contact with people the way walls do. Doors allow us to avoid codependence in our relationships and help us juggle the needs of multiple friendships and responsibilities with ease.

The process of developing close friendships and "best" friendships that the higher brain helps us achieve involves the ability to open and close these doors. When we enter the intimacy of friendship, it expands what we are capable of. When we have many walls in our boundary, we are only able to be in an *independent* state, even when we are with others, and our friendships tend to be of the lower quality, acquaintance- or friendship-of-convenience level. When we have many holes in our boundary, we are quick to find intimacy with friends, and while that feels good, it often can lock us into codependency. This too is a low-quality friendship of the type where we are briefly friends, for example, when we work in the same office, but we don't stay tight after one or the other of us changes jobs. Or we might get into such drama together that it is just too overwhelming to remain friends.

Ultimately, to find the kind of stable friendships that can be considered teamwork, partnership, and best friendship, we must make doors in our boundary, while being discriminating about what we like and accepting of what we do not. In the following diagram, when people first meet, they may notice they have a kind of *emotional* chemistry (covered in the next chapter on the mammalian brain's emotional energy). Then, as they converse, they notice that they have similar *ideas*, interests, beliefs, goals, and values. They come closer to intimacy both emotionally and intellectually. Eventually, they *decide* to do things together, and their boundaries *merge*, at least for the time they spend together. Now you have a visual model of exactly what intimacy in friendship is. It is opening your boundary to share ideas, emotions, and joint decisions with a friend.

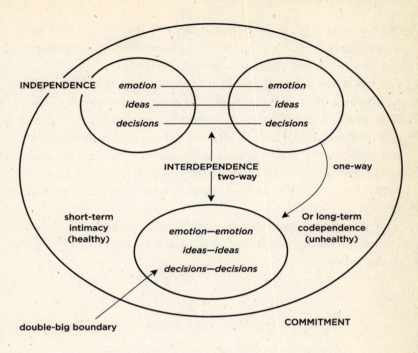

When we become stuck in a state where it feels that we cannot say no anymore, that state is *codependence*. A mature, stable friendship of high quality is built on *interdependence*—the ability to sometimes be intimate and in total agreement but also sometimes to "agree to disagree" and go off for a while being independent of each other. Too many of us fear that if we differ with our friends, we may actually lose them. But daring to have disagreements and to tolerate them is one of the hallmarks of maturity. When you take that risk, you show your friends that you will be able to handle conflict and can be relied upon to be honest, true, and loyal. If not, you are doomed to codependence and its strife, manipulation, competition, and, as a result, the frequent ending of friendships.

This is the natural course of codependent friendships that are so common with people who have a lot of boundary holes. They feel they can't say no to each other, succumb to peer pressure all the time, and eventually one person begins to gain more and more power in the relationship, using or bullying the other until eventually the resources of the less-powerful friend are depleted. The competitive and victorious "friend" then ends the friendship.

A strong personal boundary with doors prevents all this, as well as providing something beyond shared beliefs and values: shared goals.

INDEPENDENCE AGAIN

Codependence: a struggle with a winner and loser.

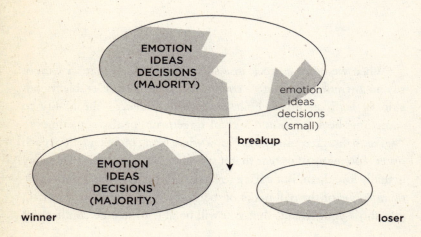

Goals, Beliefs, and Communication

Intention helps us reach goals. Goals are desired resources, rank, belonging, or achievements that are not currently in our control or owned by us. This places all goals outside our personal boundary. Yes, I realize that I said earlier that suffering amounts to trying to control things we don't control. Goals, however, though currently outside our control, will not be forever if we use our intention to go after them. Once we reach a goal, we have a new level of control in life. We have success, the extension of our control over the world around us. Just because there is much we do not now control about the world around us, does not mean that we won't someday control *more*. Goals *expand the size of our boundaries*.

Many times, teaming up with a friend who has skills that are complementary to your own, makes for the perfect team in aiming for a joint goal. In quantum psychology we all live on an intellectual spectrum, from being more of a left-brained person (logical and analytical) to being more of a right-brained person (creative,

Reaching Goals and Expanding the Boundary Size

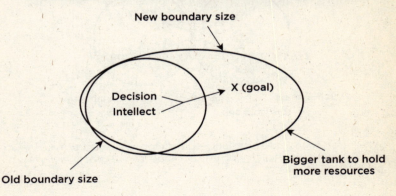

artistic, flexible, and freewheeling). We bring to mutual goals what neither friend has alone.

However, we can never, ever set goals inside another person's boundary. How many times have you had a friend that had a goal for you of, let's say, losing weight? It wasn't your goal. It was her goal *for* you. It didn't work for her, did it? How many times have you had a goal of "fixing a man" or making him more of the Prince Charming you always wanted? It didn't work, did it? How do I know this without even having met you? Because I know how boundaries work. What is inside the boundaries of others is "unalienable." We can never forcibly change people or make our success or happiness dependent on the actions of others. Never. It will not work.

When we are in a one-on-one friendship, we don't invade each other's personal territory too deeply—except once in awhile when we are at the level of best friends, partners, or in some sort of close commitment like roommates or business associates can be. Then, it

Friendship and Boundaries

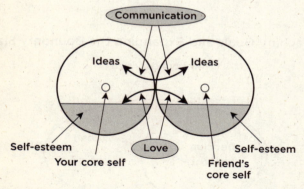

Whether through a hole or a door, and therefore regardless of maturity level, love and communication happen at the "edge" of two people's adjoining personal boundaries.

is at the mutual doors in our boundaries that we communicate and through which we "love" or donate positive emotion to each other.

Yet when we have mature boundary doors to help us collaborate, compromise, and commit to others, we can indeed have group goals that aren't inside either of our boundaries. These skills allow us to have multiple friendships that add to our social network and give us more friendship power.

Group Boundaries, Circles of Friends, and Friendship Triangles

You can grow a Seventh Sense about friendship triangles, and I teach women about this when I consult with them at www .womenshappiness.com. Say you are in a conflict with your boyfriend, but he is also a coworker at your office *and* very good friends with the male boss. How many ways can this play out for you emotionally, and what can you learn about him, yourself, and your mutual boss?

Who has negative emotion shooting out (and therefore lower value) to others? Who has their Cool Eye turned on to see what is

Friendship Triangles and Boundaries

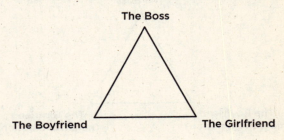

The Boss

The Boyfriend   The Girlfriend

going on from a bird's-eye view? And who does not (and therefore is more "unconscious" and at the whims of the gender-based, sur- vivalist, reptilian brain)? Who has good boundaries with doors and the ability to have different levels of friendship politics with different people at the same time?

Say you are the only one who has much of a Cool Eye turned on. You are angry with your boyfriend but still calm and "cool" about things. You can see that men bond with each other, but that doesn't have bearing on the quality of friend you can be to the boyfriend or boss. Friendship is mainly mammalian brained, not reptilian brained. This is good to know, because if you had your Cool Eye turned off, your feminine reptilian brain might feel hurt that you are excluded by their male bonding. If you also had lots of holes in your personal boundary, it would be easy to vent your hurt over the fights with your boyfriend—to yell at him at work and make yourself look bad. You might also gossip to the boss about your boyfriend, in an attempt to "belong" more to the boss's circle of friends. This would fit the normal feminine drive to belong but would leave the quality-friendship skills of your mam- malian brain and higher brain entirely out of the picture.

Friendship Triangles and Boundaries

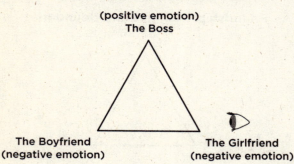

(positive emotion)
The Boss

The Boyfriend
(negative emotion)

The Girlfriend
(negative emotion)

Remember your mammalian brain and higher brain make up your character or personality. So what seems instinctual to you looks to the boss like an employee with immature boundaries, who can't keep what belongs at home, at home. He starts to consider letting you go or at least not promoting you to a leadership position.

When we are very small and more bonded to our moms than to anyone else in our lives, we are said by psychoanalysts to be competent at *dyadic relationships*. This means that we are only able to tolerate connecting with others one person at a time. This is because as small children we haven't grown mature boundaries yet. We don't see triangles between our friendships, only one line: "me" with or against the "other." We lump all others (in our example, your boyfriend and your boss) together as if they were one person.

Dyadic relationships are "linear" only

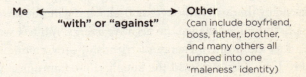

Me ←————————————————→ Other
      "with" or "against"   (can include boyfriend,
                              boss, father, brother,
                              and many others all
                              lumped into one
                              "maleness" identity)

This looks immature to the boss, and he takes the level of friendship he feels toward you down a peg. If he is mature, then he also has his Cool Eye turned on and can see with his higher brain why you are doing this. Now he is certain that your character does not merit a future leadership position at the company. Your negative emotion vented on the boss lowers your friendship level. Your character has become your destiny through friendship processes.

This looks immature on some level to the boyfriend too, and it plays out further in the level of intimacy you share. The sexual attraction he once felt for you has diminished because low character in a woman actually threatens the masculine need for secure territory, rank among other males (the boss sees him as a wimp for being with a woman who gossips about him and disrespects workplace boundaries), and power of his reptilian brain. Your negative energy vented at the boyfriend also lowers your friendship level with him. If the boyfriend turns on his Cool Eye, he might actually start thinking of breaking up with you. Once again, character has become your destiny, this time played out through a suffering friendship with your boyfriend.

None of this is to say that you were definitely "in the wrong" in the fight. We are all "in the right" in our own ways, inside our boundaries. We are all entitled to the *opinions* we hold inside our boundaries. What matters is that, whether you were right or wrong in the fight, the behavior of the boss and boyfriend are not in your control. The most you can do is keep good boundaries set about what belongs at work and what belongs at home, and metabolize your emotions, acting on them to feel better so that you can recover the positive energy that will fuel ongoing friendship with the boss. If you so choose, you might change the negative energy you feel with your boyfriend to the positive energy of friendship—by communicating with him. If he hasn't crossed the line, find a compromise you can agree on.

This would be showing ability at what psychoanalysts call *triadic relationships*, a more mature-boundaried ability to discriminate between several friendships at once, seeing each as unique and individual.

In the diagram of a triadic relationship, we see that those who have their Cool Eye turned on can see things as triadic and relate to each other with the mature boundaries of good character. When one of the involved people does not have his Cool Eye turned on (the boyfriend), the others can see the relationship as triadic while he still sees only a dyad. This means that the boyfriend would come across as a hothead to the boss and a jerk to the girlfriend,

Triadic relationships have
good boundaries with "doors"

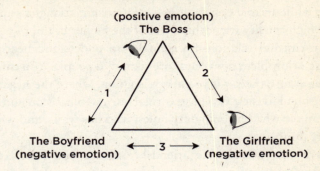

(positive emotion)
The Boss

1

2

3

The Boyfriend
(negative emotion)

The Girlfriend
(negative emotion)

and he would tend to lump both the girlfriend and the boss together as being "against him"—even if the boss had no idea about the fight. He may then project his negative feelings onto the boss through holes in his boundary and, ironically, anger the boss for real. Many people call this a *self-fulfilling prophecy*. It happens through projection and boundary holes.

In this situation, the boyfriend might call his girlfriend a bad name in front of the boss, jarring him and embarrassing the girlfriend, making her feel insecure (and therefore not sexually attracted to the man who is supposed to protect her and make her feel secure through his masculinity). His character is his destiny and plays out through suffering friendships with both his boss and his girlfriend. He may end up out of both a job and a girlfriend.

Looking at the diagram, we can see that there are actually three separate relationships. None of them have to have anything to do with the other. In everyday life, we sometimes forget this. Boyfriend's connection to girlfriend belongs at home in its drama. Boss's friendship with boyfriend is separate from his friendship with girlfriend, and if either of them rise in position faster than the other, it isn't because of personal connections. Dyadic relationships leave us at the maturity level of the reptilian and mammalian brain, while triadic connections—relationship triangles—take us to the high-quality friendship level of the higher brain.

You can use relationship triangles to understand nearly any conflict or problem between more than two people. You can literally see where the positive energy is going, where the negative is going, who has their Cool Eye turned on, and who is on autopilot. You can see who has boundary holes, who has walls, and who has mature doors.

Have you ever had a friendship where you felt like you and your friend were the same person, joined at the hip, like a giant, a force of nature made up of two bodies and minds merged as one? Then you know the intimacy of friendship. What caused this mental experience is that you actually had a *group boundary*, together, which your two individual boundaries shared for a time.

That group boundary might carry a label such as "best friendship." In other situations, the group might be called a family, or a corporation, or a marriage, or a city. In human groups there can be boundaries around boundaries around boundaries, all of which work by the same mechanisms that an individual boundary does, with holes, walls, and doors, projection, perfectionism, lying, manipulation, and codependence.

Once you understand what we have learned so far, you can go on to managing your position within a group boundary one might call your *circle of friends*.

In any circle of friends, there will tend to be at least a leader (if it is a group of women only) or perhaps even a ranked hierarchy of friends (when men are also present). Usually, the size of the individual's boundary and how full it is of ideas, self-esteem's positive energy, and wise decision making, are what determines the rank or importance of that individual within the group. In

A Circle of Friends

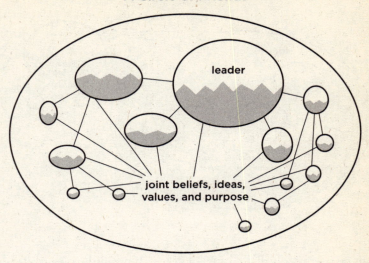

other words, the importance of each member is determined by the maturity of their character. Ideally, the person with the largest boundary, the fullest tank of positive emotion, self-esteem, and wisdom, is the leader of the group.

Within this group, each individual needs to maintain their own personal needs and boundary while at the same time sharing a common cause, set of beliefs, and values. There is a purpose to the circle, even if it is only to have occasional dinners together to chat about nothing in particular. If a member of the circle does not buy into the group interests, goals, beliefs, or values, that person will eventually be excluded from the group.

Within circles of friends, whether a family, a company, or a whole nation, there are also relationship triangles that operate by the rules we covered earlier. One's social life is a complex geometry of triangles within circles within triangles within circles. We

Scapegoating and a Dysfunctional Circle of Friends

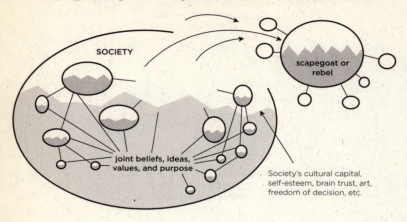

can be part of a little set of triangles, a clique within the circle of a company, while also being in a triangle that includes the circle of our family, even while our family and our company are also in triangles with other groups, and then other even larger groups' circles, such as a community, city, or nation. It is a beautiful geometric mosaic of invisible, secret psychology.

In the mini-society that we call a circle of friends, when someone goes too far astray from the main interests of the group, away from their goals or values or purpose for being, that person can be scapegoated or considered a rebel and excluded from the group. When the scapegoat is the leader of the group, this is often disastrous and splinters the whole group. How often have you seen this effect when a marriage dissolves and each partner tries to take his or her friends to the exclusion of the other partner? The whole circle can splinter.

There is power in numbers in any circle and on any team. When there is a weak link in the chain—someone of immature character or with big boundary holes or any of the group effects of projection, perfectionism, dishonesty, manipulation, codependence or any other immature boundary trait—it can be disastrous not just for an individual friend but for all in the community. I was a first responder as a psychiatrist to the Columbine tragedy and saw this community effect firsthand. Large-scale personal boundary education can minimize the impact of violence on a community through the power of quality community friendships.

You also have the power to be a leader in your circle of friends or on your team of friends. You can be an innovator even if you are not the absolute leader. You can stretch the group to try out new goals and purposes if they are not too wildly outside the beliefs and values the group now holds. This prevents you from being a scapegoat who is excluded and makes you someone who betters the entire group.

A Circle of Friends

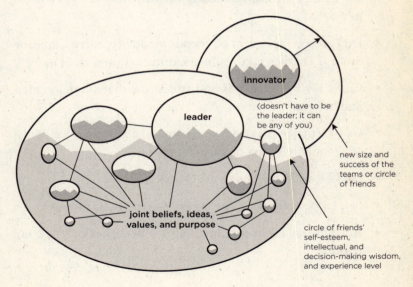

innovator

(doesn't have to be the leader; it can be any of you)

leader

new size and success of the teams or circle of friends

joint beliefs, ideas, values, and purpose

circle of friends' self-esteem, intellectual, and decision-making wisdom, and experience level

The Checklist for Friendship Quality and Numbers

- Go over your master checklist. If any of the four items are missing, it is a friendship in trouble.

- Does my friend make me feel uncomfortable, embarrassed, or seem to want me to act in ways that cause me these negative feelings? (Do I feel peer pressure?)

- Do I do this to others?

- Am I destructive (selfish, win-lose) in my decisions among friends? Are they to me?

- Do I regularly use my Cool Eye? Do my friends? Am I "cool"? Are they?

- Do I suffer (worry, complain, or use the word *should*) or make my friends suffer? Do they do it to me?

- Do I put up walls too much with friends? Do they do it to me?

- Do I get too dependent on friends for advice, energy, time, or money? Do they take too much of these things from me?

- Can I say no to friends and still know that I am accepted and belong?

- Can I let friends say no to me and take it with grace, without totally rejecting or excluding them?

- Do I lie or do they lie to me often?

- Am I a perfectionist? Are my friends too perfectionist?

- Am I in denial about anything in my behavior? Are my friends?

- Do I ever catch myself projecting onto friends—blaming them for faults I don't like about myself? Do my friends project onto me?

- Am I over-independent, codependent, or interdependent with my friends?

- Do I set goals inside my friends' boundaries? Do they do that too often to me?

- Can I work on a team or be comfortable agreeing to most of the ideas, beliefs, or purposes of my circle of friends? Do they accept my ideas and beliefs?

- Am I a leader among my friends or am I passive? Is my group itself too passive and lacking leadership?

- Am I a sufferer or someone with mature intentions for myself and others?

- Are my potential friends sufferers, or are they people with mature intentions?

Chapter Four

The Real Secret: The Mammalian Brain and Friendship

The greatest good you can do for another is not just to share your riches but to reveal to him his own.
—BENJAMIN DISRAELI

WE NOW understand two ends of the friendship spectrum: the reptilian brain (immature, closer to "stranger," survival based) and the higher brain (mature, committed, closer to "best friend," team based). In quantum psychology, if we have a grasp of the two ends of any spectrum of behavior, we can easily solve any problem in between. We can enrich our lives no matter who we are or what backgrounds our friends come from, and we can be unique people while understanding the secret workings of all of friendship in general. It is time to dive into the very heart of friendship. The core of all friendship—whether casual and temporary or committed and lifelong—is the positive emotional energy of the mammalian brain.

The only energy that humans possess, that they can manipulate to create happiness and success in their lives, and that they can learn to manage consciously, is the energy called self-esteem. Self-esteem is a positive emotional energy that flows through the process we call friendship. Friendship is your one special power in life and self-esteem is its *fuel*.

I have never in my professional life known a chronically depressed or anxious person who had durable self-esteem; nor have

I known a person with durable self-esteem who ever got depressed or anxious for long. Self-esteem directly correlates to our moods, how positively or negatively others perceive us, and ultimately how effective we will be in forming and keeping friendships. The human instinct to form friendships evolved originally because there was a high survival value in "circling the wagons"—strength in numbers. We have friendships because we need something and, in simplest terms, that something is called self-esteem.

Self-esteem (positive emotional energy) = Well-being + Confidence

We are not *emotionally attracted* to people who have low self-esteem. On an instinctual level, we feel that they might somehow lower our standing in a group, cause us to become outcasts, or even bring our mood down. Somewhere inside ourselves, we know that these people belong in the category "not friend." The low self-esteem of others causes them to be depressive, passive-aggressive, threatening, violent, harsh, insulting, worrisome, to play the victim, complain, or to be impulsive and addictive. These are the very things that stress us, and we know that stress is the ultimate enemy of friendship, a negative energy that comes from outside our boundary to attack our mood.

Stress (negative emotional energy) = Hurt + Loss

If stress gets into our friendships, it is poison. When we have weak boundaries with holes in them, the stresses of life can get in more easily. We call this *unhappiness*, and with our Cool Eye turned on, may find ourselves thinking, "I'm unhappy in this friendship." This unhappiness results from stress draining away our self-esteem. The new unhappiness also has two forms.

Unhappiness (the enemy of friendship) = Anger + Anxiety

If hurt gets into us, it drains away some of our well-being, and we feel *anger*. If loss (depletion) gets into us, it drains away some of our confidence, and we feel *anxiety*. If you have ever had a friend who couldn't control her anger very well, you probably found yourself feeling consistently unhappy around her and the friendship probably died. If you ever had a friend who was always worrying *at* you, dumping her negative energy into your boundary and draining away your confidence, you probably felt consistently unhappy and that friendship probably died as well. Our misman-agement of anger and anxiety are the ultimate roadblocks to stable friendships.

Remember your master checklist. Friendship requires *consistent, mutual, shared positive emotion*. Carrying around resent-ment, depression, bitterness, worry, complaints, irritability, severe

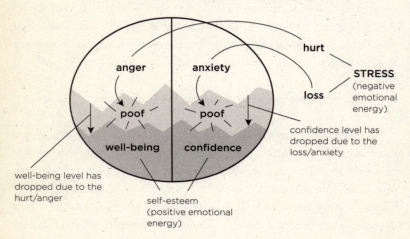

Relationship of Stress and Self-esteem

hurt

anger   anxiety

STRESS
(negative
emotional
energy)

loss

poof   poof

confidence level has
dropped due to the
loss/anxiety

well-being   confidence

well-being level has
dropped due to the
hurt/anger

self-esteem
(positive emotional
energy)

sarcasm, hopelessness, helplessness, or any other variants of what amount to just two things—anger or anxiety—are sure friendship killers. We need a way to fix these.

Because of what you have already learned about boundaries, you know that you have the power to correct these problems in yourself. You can also offer help to longtime friends in a way that fits your time budget, schedule, and the amount of energy you have to give away. Be careful, though, to avoid becoming everyone's therapist or substitute parent. That is the same as codependence.

We are going to learn the ultimate secrets of human energy in this chapter. This is what science has said for a hundred years—if not thousands—about the impact of mood on friendship. It turns out that anger and anxiety are the *only* two purely negative emotions. Just as all colors are combinations of the three primary colors—red, yellow, and blue—your negative emotions are some combination of anger and anxiety. Once again, quantum psychology requires us to see a human trait on a spectrum with two ends and then find our unique, specific place on that spectrum to enjoy our individuality.

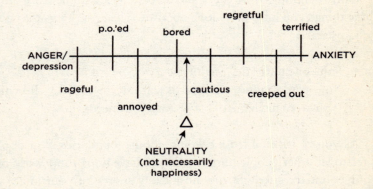

Whatever word you use, every uncomfortable emotion
you ever feel exists somewhere on this spectrum.

You'll notice that anger and depression (sadness) are on the same end of the spectrum. This is because they are the same emotion. Anyone you have ever seen weep might have told you she was sad or angry. Some early psychoanalysts even described depression as *anger turned inward*. If you look at the spectrum previous, though, you'll be able to see that when you are not feeling good your mood will fall somewhere in the range between pure anger/sadness and pure anxiety. No matter where we are on this spectrum at any given time, it is bad for friendship because it harms the core element of our master definition of friendship.

We obviously need to address this. At the website where I help women, www.womenshappiness.com, I give you the fine details of the ways we can correct our anger and anxiety problems. Here we will stick to the basics.

The Anger Map

Only two things have ever caused you anger, and there are only three things you have ever done about it. The two things that got you upset are:

- Someone hurt you (one of the two types of stress)
- You were low on the type of self-esteem called well-being (you were having trouble getting your needs met)

As you've learned from reading about boundaries, you don't *have* to let other people hurt you. If you have done some work on your boundary strength, the most likely source of your anger is that you are simply not getting your needs met very well in life.

Well-being is the type of energy that is nurturing, "motherly,"

Anger Map

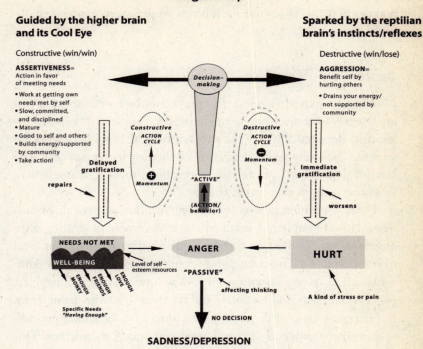

Guided by the higher brain and its Cool Eye

Constructive (win/win)

ASSERTIVENESS= Action in favor of meeting needs

• Work at getting own needs met by self
• Slow, committed, and disciplined
• Mature
• Good to self and others
• Builds energy/supported by community
• Take action!

Delayed gratification

repairs

Decision-making

Constructive ACTION CYCLE

⊕ *Momentum*

"ACTIVE"

(ACTION/ behavior)

Sparked by the reptilian brain's instincts/reflexes

Destructive (win/lose)

AGGRESSION= Benefit self by hurting others

• Drains your energy/ not supported by community

Destructive ACTION CYCLE

⊖ *Momentum*

Immediate gratification

worsens

NEEDS NOT MET

WELL-BEING

ENOUGH MONEY   ENOUGH FRIENDS   ENOUGH LOVE

Specific Needs "Having Enough"

Level of self— esteem resources

ANGER

"PASSIVE"

affecting thinking

NO DECISION

HURT

A kind of stress or pain

SADNESS/DEPRESSION

In the mammalian brain or emotional brain

and smooths the workings of your life. If you are angry, chances are you don't now feel enough nurturing in your life or have not had enough consistent *mothering* from others prior to now. You will eventually need to go get your own needs met efficiently if you are to be a good friend to others, and those who rely too much on you to meet their needs (instead of doing it for themselves) will eventually tire you out.

All you have ever been able to do with your anger is to transform it into three types of behavior: *depression, aggression,* or *assertiveness.* None of these is inherently bad. They are in all of us to greater or lesser extents, and they have their purposes. It's just that the first two sink your friendships while assertiveness actually builds them.

Depression

When you are depressed, you make a poor friend because you are telegraphing negative energy to others. People can become biologically depressed, where the hardware of the brain isn't working so well. They may need medication or therapy to get out of it. The level of depression I am talking about here, though, is one where you have sadness that repels friends.

There is nothing inherently wrong with having periods of sadness. This is simply the mammalian brain's way of dealing with anger—a signal telling us there is something wrong with our level of resources. We have needs, and when they are not met, our emotions call us to pay attention, to review how we got to this place, process old hurts and traumas, and try to take lessons from them. But carrying around depression or sadness for extended periods, and exposing others to it, consistently sabotages friendships. This is unfortunate since most depressed people could really use friends more than anything else in life.

Aggression

Aggression harms others or it is not aggression. Aggression is also not inherently bad. It is simply the reptilian brain's option for processing our anger, since the reptilian brain's absolute duty is to protect our survival. In ages past, when we were in great need of food or under attack from the aggression of others, we often needed to run on pure survival instinct. Aggression lacks conscious self-awareness. This is why many people with aggression problems say that it is as if something just took over their bodies when they act this way.

Aggression is a "quick fix" for anger. It makes us feel good temporarily because we have taken the negative energy in ourselves and dumped it into someone else's boundary. Our anger leaves our boundary through a hole, causes hurt to someone (either going through a hole in her boundary or busting in against her wishes, which is called *trauma*). Now it sits in the other person, as new anger that person feels. You feel *better*, she feels *worse*, and that is why all aggression is a win-lose (and immature) method of dealing with anger.

You've heard of the "kick the dog syndrome." This is where we have a bad day and take it out on others. We come home and "kick the dog." This syndrome is never okay in a friendship. A destructive choice, a win-lose way to treat people, it amounts to using our friends as a dumping ground. This was our mode with our parents when we were children, and if they raised us with maturity, good boundaries, and wisdom, we eventually learned that it is not okay to dump our angry feelings on others by hurting them.

Assertiveness

Assertiveness is not dumping on or hurting others for your benefit. It is a win-win, constructive mode of dealing with your anger, and it actually transforms anger into something good. Assertiveness uses your anger as energy to get your needs met without hurting, using, manipulating, or disrespecting others. Finding the ability to be assertive is a decidedly mature skill, one powered by the higher brain, with its good boundary management; wise, constructive decisions; and Cool Eye.

Assertiveness is always good for a friendship because it shows that you are willing to own your problems and needs, that you can be trusted to "pull your own weight," and that you have the power to be a good, mutual, sharing teammate in the life of the friendship. Through assertiveness, you can actually take negative emotional energy (anger) and transform it into positive emotional energy (well-being), which is the very fuel of friendship.

If you are in need of a better job, you don't have to whine and moan to your friends about your current job. They will tire of this. You don't have to take it out on them by insulting them or being bitter. You don't have to make them uncomfortable by being jealous of them (jealousy is a form of aggression). You simply need to be assertive—patiently, persistently, and maturely—with a goal of finding yourself a better career path. Do the work of making a great résumé, or take classes to prepare you for a change.

In the end, no friend can live your life for you, get the job of your dreams for you, or be responsible for the actions you are not taking in your life. Assertiveness amounts to *mothering yourself* when there isn't a mother around for you. Assertiveness is the key to cultivating all the well-being you want. You'll even have some excess that you can give away by mothering your friends when they need it.

The Anxiety Map

Only two things have ever caused you anxiety, and you have only ever done three things about it. The two things that got you upset are:

- Someone caused you *loss* (the second of the two types of stress)
- You were low on the type of self-esteem called confidence (you lacked the feeling that you could tolerate risk, change, or loss)

In your friendships, you don't *have* to let other people threaten you or cause you to lose resources. If you have done some work on your boundary strength, the most likely source of your anxiety is that you are simply low on confidence against threats or challenges, or about the need for risk and changes in life.

What is confidence? Confidence is the type of energy that gets things done even in the face of risk, change, or potential loss. It is "fatherly" and powers the need for taking action in your life. It is "knowing you can do it." Even for the most wealthy, nurtured person, it is only confidence that gives them the ability to *use* their resources and put their *potential* into *action*.

If you are anxious, chances are it is because you have had experiences of loss in the past or don't feel enough go-getter spirit in your life. If you are often anxious and do not have a diagnosed anxiety disorder, you have not had the experience of feeling consistently *fathered* by the authority figures and mentors in your life. You will eventually need to take independent risks in life if you are to be a good friend to others, and those who rely too much on you to pump up their confidence (instead of doing it for themselves) will eventually tire you out.

All you have ever been able to do with your anxiety is to transform it into three types of behavior: *impulsiveness/avoidance, victim thinking (masochism)*, and *courage*. All of these are in us to greater or lesser extents, and they have their purposes. It's just that the first two sink your friendships while the third actually builds them.

Impulsiveness/Avoidance

When you are impulsive, overly shy, or avoidant, you make a poor friend because you telegraph negative energy to others who are, or want to be, your friend. As with depression, there are certainly biological contributors that can be present. Reasons for impulsiveness can include closed head injuries, attention deficit disorder, and other conditions where the hardware of the brain isn't working so well. These people might need medication or therapy. The level of impulsiveness I am talking about here, though, is one where you have psychological or personality-based impulsiveness or shyness that repels friends.

There is nothing inherently wrong about having periods of impulsiveness, such as when you go on the very rare shopping spree. This is simply the reptilian brain's way of dealing with anxiety. Very long ago, if we didn't have the survival instinct to respond impulsively to a threat, we would die. We know this as the "fight or flight" reflex, designed to save our lives. However, today it is rare that there is an immediate threat to our survival. Yet the fight or flight reflex shows up when our anxiety gets to such a level that we have *panic attacks*. In other ways, too, this reflex can harm us, such as when we quell our anxieties with addictions of all kinds (food, drugs, alcohol, shopping, or gambling). The natural tendency of anxiety is to drive us into impulsive action if we don't use some higher-brain Cool Eye self-observation and attention to boundaries.

Impulsiveness is a signal that tells us something is wrong with our environment and that we need to pay attention to risks and challenges, review the past, process old losses and traumas, and try to take lessons from them. However, being impulsive or running away from our problems for extended periods, and exposing others to this, sabotages friendships.

Victim Thinking (Masochism)

The second option for anxiety is "playing the victim" or *masochism*. Masochism harms you and/or others or it is not masochism. Masochism is also not inherently bad. It is simply the mammalian brain's option for processing anxiety without the help of the higher brain's maturity. In friendship, the mammalian brain is responsible only for emotional bonding and nothing more so-phisticated than that without the help of the higher brain. Yet if you combine the mammalian brain's function with the reptilian brain's absolute duty of protecting our survival, you see some-thing very interesting.

When we were children, we often acted helpless: playing the victim fearful of monsters under the bed, or acting (and possibly being) too weak to lift our bicycle over the fence. We cried and whined and whimpered, and it turns out this had a very positive purpose for our survival. It actually caused sympathy in adults; it was cute, endearing, and bonded them to us, which all children need for survival's sake. Yet once we come into adulthood, this survival reflex, still paired with our mammalian brain's bonding ability, doesn't look nearly as cute anymore. Adults start to shun or avoid other adults who play the victim or are masochistic.

Masochism is an emotional habit in us that, like aggression, lacks conscious self-awareness.

Masochism is a "quick fix" for our anxiety, and that makes it tempting to use often. When we lean on others; borrow their con-fidence; or dump our worries, complaints, hopeless and helpless feelings, or any other form of anxiety into them, we at least tem-porarily feel good. Why? Because we have taken the negative en-ergy in ourselves and dumped it into someone else's boundary. Our anxiety leaves our boundary through a hole, causes someone to feel our loss (either going through a hole in her boundary or bust-ing in against her wishes, guilting her in passive-aggressiveness, which is still called *trauma*). Now it sits in the other person, as new anxiety *she* feels. We feel *better*, she feels *worse*, and that is why all masochism, or playing the victim, is a win-lose (and immature) method of dealing with anxiety.

Masochism is never okay in a friendship. It is subtle because it is not an outward action in the way that aggressive acts are. Many masochistic people tend to make you feel as if their worry and victimization is somehow your fault, or at least your responsibility to handle *for* them. Since the nature of friendship is one of sharing and mutuality, it is tempting to become caught up in another's masochism. Yet as a destructive behavior, a win-lose way to treat people, playing the victim masochistically amounts to using our friends as a dumping ground.

Courage

The third and only other thing you have ever done with anxiety is to transform it into *courage*. Courage never involves dumping on others or making them feel guilty for your benefit. It is a win-win, constructive mode of dealing with your anxiety by actually transforming it to good ends. Courage is going out and *using your anxiety as an energy* to face your fears and do the right thing, without guilt-tripping, using, manipulating, or disrespecting others. Finding the ability to be courageous is a decidedly mature skill, powered by the higher brain.

Through courage, you can take negative emotional energy (anxiety) and transform it into positive emotional energy (confidence), which is the very fuel of action in friendship. The only time to avoid using courage is when there is a truly life-threatening situation upon you. In that case, let your reptilian brain panic, preserve your life by impulsively running away, and live to take calculated risks another day.

If you are facing a personal challenge, job loss, divorce, health problem, addiction, or simply the need for a new life change toward growth and maturity, remember it is *your* life to live. Friends are a bonus. They are not there to find the answers for you. Courage is essentially *fathering yourself* when there is not a fatherly person around you.

You've now learned to address the other end of the spectrum of negative energy and how to transform it to positive energy. Now you are fully equipped to take any stress on friendship or on your personal life, any negative emotion you carry (which brings down your ability to make friendships), and instead create a life of self-esteem through cultivating the only two actions that can create it out of nothing: assertiveness and courage.

The complete Anxiety Map looks like this:

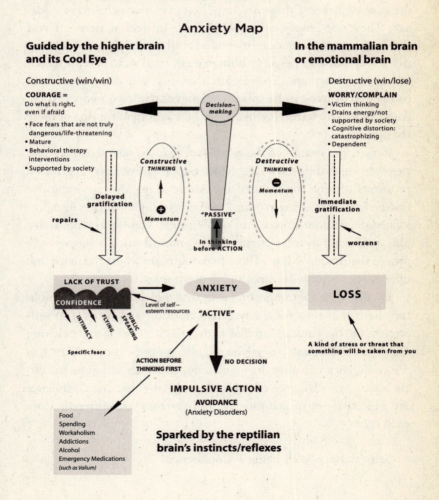

Anxiety Map

You'll notice that there is a certain symmetry in the Anger Map and the Anxiety Map. They both have outside stress as a potential cause. Yet hurt and loss, while both types of stress, are different from each other. Both maps also have three possible directions in which you can channel the negative emotion. In the case of anger, these are depression, aggression, or assertiveness, while in the case of anxiety, these are impulsiveness, masochism, or courage. These are emotional states that we all feel at times. If you use both maps in tandem to understand yourself, you will find that every possible negative human emotional state is represented somewhere on them. This means that any and every emotional problem we have can be solved. Whatever name you apply to the emotion you now feel, it will always be a synonym for one of these six options.

In fact, the beauty of the emotional maps is also that they link together three-dimensionally. Most people who have aggression problems (on the top right of the Anger Map) also are impulsive (lower arm of the Anxiety Map), and most people who get into prolonged depressions (lower arm of the Anger Map) also tend to display a tendency to feel victimized or act masochistically (upper right arm of the Anxiety Map). These two points are where the maps link up: aggression/impulsiveness and depression/masochism.

Finally, both maps are similar in that they lead you to one solitary path that resolves the negative emotion and turns it to self-esteem. On the Anger Map that path is the well-being you cultivate for yourself through assertiveness, and on the Anxiety Map it is the confidence you gain through courage. Which brings us full circle back to our $E = mc^2$ of psychology. Well-being and confidence are indeed types of self-esteem, and yet they are different from each other.

Self-esteem = Well-being + Confidence

To be complete, you need equal measures of both. That is why we need two maps, not one. When you use them together, you can solve any emotional problem you have had or will ever have.

The Only Thing of Value and the Only People We Love

Think of a diamond, a car, your bank account, your home, your city, the weather, your husband, or your boyfriend. Think of past boyfriends, your family, or your best friend. What makes these more or less valuable?

Consider what it is like to live with a roommate you hardly ever see, with whom you have nothing in common except the legal document you signed in order to take the lease. You have a commitment, legally, but does that mean you love or value that person as anything more than someone who pays half the rent? No, you can't possibly love or value that person unless there is something more to your connection to each other. That missing thing is friendship, and in this case the commitment you have is mediated only by the higher brain and its diplomatic agreements that respect the rights of the citizens of your community. Valuing people as more than an abstraction does not exist in the higher brain.

On the other end of the spectrum, consider what it is like to be on a date with someone who only seems to want to sleep with you right away. Does this person love you? Of course not. Love takes time. Does this person value you? Again, of course not. Lust and desire are purely reptilian-brain experiences and valuing does not exist in the reptilian brain.

There are two parts to love and value. Loving someone, and value itself, are located only in the mammalian brain's emotional centers. For us to love someone or something there needs to be an

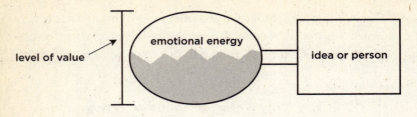

Value = amount of emotional energy
attached to a person or idea

object of that love, whether this is a person, pet, or possession. There also needs to be a *measured amount of emotional energy* that we attach to that object or person.

If you use this diagram in various areas of your life, you'll be able to come to quicker decisions about what actions to take in your friendships, career, romantic life, and virtually everything else that matters. It illustrates yet another reason why the system of friendship is the real secret to success and happiness: when we devote our time, energy, money, or any other resource to activities with good boundaries, we are most efficient and productive when we do so for the things, people, and ideas we most *value*.

Have you ever taken a job that you felt good about at first but that ultimately left you with a sense that something was very wrong? Perhaps the mission of the company went against what you believe in politically or spiritually, or you ultimately found the product or service you delivered boring. Within months or, tragically, *years*, you realized that you were on the wrong path in life, but everything seemed vague when you considered what to do next. Why?

Because you didn't stop to wonder what you value. That is to say that the activities, ideas, and people of the company were not of value to you; you didn't have positive emotions attached to the ideas, people, or mission of the company. For all its good intentions, the company did not give you value back in positive energy that is relevant to the ideas, people, or things you really do *care* about. The money you made did not add up to the amount of energy, time, and effort you put toward something that doesn't match your values. It is a win-lose deal for you psychologically and spiritually even if you make a million dollars a year.

Have you ever been in the same situation with a romance or a friend? You did your best to be yourself and to give time, energy, money, and your concern to this person, but what you valued did not at all match what *the other person* valued. I have seen this countless times in the office, where a romantic couple, a family, or a pair of friends come to me to tell me how they "give and give and give" to each other. When I ask *what* they give, the answer clarifies problem.

"I gave her a diamond necklace for Christmas," the man says. "I gave him a subscription to *Sports Illustrated*," she says. "I gave my mom a new watch," he says. "I gave my son a nice arts-and-crafts set," Mom says. "I gave my friend a book I really liked," she says. When we give gifts, we like to think that we are connecting, giving, and loving, but if we give the gift of conversation, presents, behavior, or anything else that the other person doesn't value, their perception of it is not love, kindness, or any value at all. Forget "it's the thought that counts." It doesn't count much to the mammalian brain if the wife values hugs far more than diamonds, the man values *Esquire* far more than *Sports Illustrated*, your mom is retired and cares less about telling time than going on a vacation, your son likes trucks rather than art, or you enjoy murder mysteries but your friend detests them.

The common denominator is that whatever gifts we give or interactions we have, if we are not giving value in the form of items, gestures, words, or behaviors that actually transmit feelings of higher self-esteem into the psyche of the other person, we are not loving them, and we are thus not valued *by* them or valuable *to* them. Friends are indispensable to each other not because of neediness (a desire that is usually fleeting or unpredictable), nor because of commitments rendered on legal documents, but only because of our ability to raise self-esteem.

Love is the currency of emotional value in our lives. It is a gauge of positive emotion in the mammalian brain, one that tells us how much we are worth other than in dollars, what the other person is worth in units of pleasure, not in money, and what level of friendship we share. Love is not a decision, nor is it a contract. It is free of promises and obligations. It isn't a manifesto or a zap of lustful lightning. It is simply a flush of self-esteem, a measure of our happiness in connection to those we love.

Love as a currency can be "traded" for other resources. When we bake cookies with love, we are exchanging currencies with the person who will eventually eat the cookies and find that they feel good to eat. When a nurse spends her positive emotional energy on a patient, the patient doesn't give her a gift—but perhaps he tells her boss what a difference she made, and that might ultimately lead to a raise. The original value of her love flowed through various human media, to transform into money in her bank account.

In the mindOS system of psychology, I represent the four kinds of currencies we exchange with each other as being attached to the four kinds of inner resources in our psychology:

The Currencies of Love, Time, and Freedom

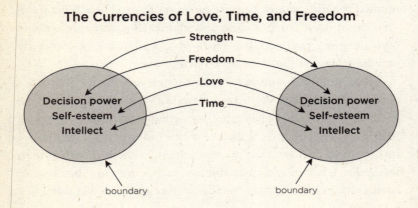

When we lend strength by protecting a friend with our stronger boundary, we are giving value that might spur the other to feel love in exchange, to value us. When we spend our time on someone, as in conversation or teaching or listening where ideas are exchanged, we may receive love in return. When we give up some of our freedom, as in trusting a mentor to make decisions for us or listening to the wisdom of our parent, we may receive love in return for the control we have surrendered. And, of course, nothing is as directly reciprocal as giving love, raising another's self-esteem, and finding that that person feels compelled to do the same in return.

This is the invisible psychology of friendship: when we cause an elevation of self-esteem in others that is directly and exclusively linked to *us*, we are immediately, automatically valued. The person is then our friend, and she brings more and more value into our lives, which we can then send back out again. The secret is not "it's the thought that counts." It is the *emotion* that counts. The positive emotion we inspire in others.

Beliefs and Communication

Two other things are closely attached to the emotional energy and feeling of value in the mammalian brain. These are *beliefs* and *communication*. A belief is a dearly held idea, an opinion rather than a scientific fact. This is one of the prime reasons that we have had a thousand-year history of disagreement between science and the church. Inside her boundaries, every person is perfectly entitled to believe what she wants, but when we get into scientific inquiry, the facts that result from experimentation force us all to come to the same conclusions, opinions, and belief about a matter. This might be frustrating to us, for we value our beliefs highly. If we get feedback from the environment that clashes with what we believe, it threatens the positive emotional energy we attach to our beliefs—unless we learn how to use boundaries effectively. Likewise, when we converse with friends, we find that communication is also an idea attached to emotional energy. What makes communication different from belief is that it is information (ideas) and energy in transit to others, as opposed to just sitting inside our boundary.

Sharing beliefs is important to friendships. The emotionless ideas of the higher brain may not have much bearing on the quality of our friendships, but our emotion-laden beliefs, which form anchors of connection between the higher brain and the mammalian brain, most certainly have a profound effect on friendships.

There was once an experiment conducted among college students about how much we "like" others. A physically attractive male model entered a room and sat down. The research subjects were told to rate his "likeability." At first, on a scale of one to ten, the students gave him an average rating of slightly more than six. His good looks were so far above those of the average person that it was difficult to relate to or like him. Yet when he was asked to enter the room, sit down, and spill coffee on himself, his likeability score went far up, to an eight or nine out of ten. The message of this experiment is that we like the most those with whom we feel the greatest similarity. Nowhere is this more effectively explained than in this visual model of a belief.

A belief is much like a tabletop supported by legs that we could call *evidence*. The surface of the belief itself is an idea, or statement, such as "I am a loser" or "I am a good person" or "pizza is delicious." The idea or statement itself does not carry much weight or value in our lives until we find that we have had experiences connected with the idea—experiences that carry emotional energy, whether positive (happiness) or negative (anger or anxiety or both). You can envision these packets of positive or negative emotional energy as being like superglue that locks a belief to the "floor" of your mind. The emotion makes a belief durable. This is

Beliefs Are Like a Tabletop: Supported by Legs Called "Evidence"

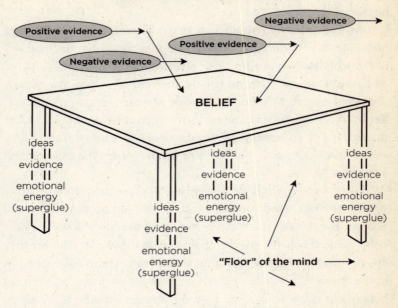

Thousands of beliefs are locked to the "floor" of an individual's mind and compose the sum total of what is termed one's reality, worldview, or frame of reference.

If the majority of these beliefs is composed of beliefs with positive energy, then the individual's overall worldview is a positive one. If the majority of these beliefs is composed of beliefs with negative energy, then the individual's overall worldview is a negative one.

As a belief grows in strength and dominance, it becomes more facile at collecting positive evidence, e.g. evidence that the belief is true, rejecting negative evidence, e.g. evidence that the belief is untrue.

why when we have a friend who is down and out over a job loss, for example, she seems immune and resistant to all our encouragements about what a good person she is and how much she has going for her. These sentiments are like throwing roses at a fire.

The friend may understand our support with her higher brain, but the deep negative emotion connected to the job loss locks down her belief that she is "a loser."

Imagine that your mind is a floor. Thousands of beliefs are locked to that floor, and compose the sum total of your "reality" or "worldview"—your frame of reference.

If the majority of those beliefs are held with positive energy, then your overall worldview is a positive one. You are an optimist. Yet if, like many people, the majority of your beliefs are locked to the surface of your mind by negative energy, your overall worldview is a negative one. You are a pessimist (or maybe call yourself a "realist").

Either way—optimist or pessimist—all those thousands of tables resting on your mind form the surface that supports your mental activity. For this reason, it can be very hard to change someone's beliefs. We need beliefs to navigate our way in the world, whether they are positive or negative. Without them, we become disoriented or even entirely lost. We don't know who we are anymore. So for most people it is easier to hang on to being a pessimist who is certain of who she is than to be confused, immobile, and without the ability to predict what may happen next. This is why, when you go to console a great friend—someone who seems to have everything going for her but is depressed or anxious—she will tell you that she understands in her head how good she has it, but she just can't feel it in her heart. It can be a futile struggle to change a friend's emotions by simply using logic. Emotions do not work by higher-brain logic. They work by the invisible psychology of the mammalian brain.

Yet here's the catch. Beliefs can't exist unless they are supported by the "table legs," or evidence. As a belief, whether positive or negative, gains strength and dominance over your mind, it becomes more effective at collecting additional evidence that it is true and rejecting or automatically ignoring any evidence to the contrary.

Our minds need to work this way for the sake of efficiency. We wouldn't be able to go about doing the smallest task—brushing our teeth, for example—if we always had to take the time to reassess what is true or untrue about the world around us. If we couldn't believe from day to day that the toothbrush in our bathroom was really a toothbrush, we'd never even get the things in our mouths.

You're ready to move on to what's next in your day only because of the artificial sense of certainty that your beliefs give you. Still, as you can clearly see in the diagram above, there is just as much evidence in the environment to disprove your beliefs as there is to support them. These efficient, helpful parts of our personal reality are only opinions. They can never be absolute scientific facts, and that is the source of so much of the strife in friendships. For our beliefs, our opinions, can never be worth more—or be "more right"—than those of our friends.

If you were to step outside yourself and look at all the negative beliefs you have about yourself (some call these "disempowering" beliefs and psychoanalysts call them "negative cognitions"), you may find that there is more negativity in you than you ever realized. It can be reflected in the things we say to ourselves, as when we trip over a curb and erupt, "I'm so stupid!" With your Cool Eye turned on, though, you can objectively look at yourself and say, "It was just an accident, not an excuse to beat up on myself, and it really is a different situation from those times in the past when I felt stupid."

Because our beliefs not only carry the emotion of the mammalian brain but also the information we store in the higher brain, they have a dual and profound importance on friendships. We tend to form friendships with those who share our beliefs about major issues in life (religion, politics, socioeconomic cultural preferences, etc.). Yet because positive emotional energy is the very core of friendship, even people who have similar hobbies and interests may not make very good friends if their beliefs bring negative energy to the interests you share. Ultimately, it is far easier to like a person and call her a friend, even if she has opposite ideas to our own, if the association with that person brings you positive emotion. This is what makes many public speakers so enticing: they make us feel good by emotionally appealing to the mammalian brain's sense of friendship, even if we disagree stridently with their ideas.

Since we only control what is inside our boundary, we would do well to turn on the Cool Eye and use it to observe what negative beliefs we might want to develop evidence *against*. At the same time, we might want to develop new, more empowering beliefs that embody positive energy. For example, if your friend lost her job, she would serve herself well to recall all the successful jobs she had in the past, relive the good emotions attached to those positive experiences, and feel the salve of memory on her new wound. She also might seek out new jobs she is likely to be successful in, and which will bring her new experiences with positive emotion in them. These will then form new beliefs about her competence in her career and will lock them to the floor of her mind with high-self-esteem superglue.

Our beliefs limit our perception. We can only see information about us and about the world that already fits what we believe. We don't see both sides of the coin but instead only see the one that we already believe. If you look at the belief diagram again, you'll see both positive, supporting data and negative, differing data floating over the table surface of a belief. The more emotionally charged and valued the belief we have, the stronger a filter of reality it becomes. In order to squelch a negative belief, then, we need a new belief with positive energy to stamp out the negative one.

Since the structure of a strong belief essentially blinds us to all the options the environment's evidence might offer, you need your Cool Eye here. Take a realistic look at what you believe. Is it an absolute? Or is there possibly evidence for more empowering beliefs you could allow yourself to entertain?

This is crucial for friendship, and makes friendship the real secret of success and happiness. It is up to us to decide what beliefs to have and, with their positive energy, to expand the success and happiness of others as we do so for ourselves. Remember, "character is destiny" is the only law of success and happiness.

The friendship process doesn't leave beliefs just sitting inside our boundaries. We communicate our beliefs to others through language, our bodies, and our observed behavior. Communication is a very interesting thing. In this day of great feats of telecommunication technology, of texting and e-mail, we might be tempted to think of it as merely data. But that is not all communication is. Communication has value too. Think of how you feel when you get a handwritten letter from an old friend or a holiday card from a long-lost relative. Communication is both *data* and *energy*.

If I were to call you on a cell phone, I would indeed be sending data to you, and my cost would be the time it took to make the call. However, what happens if my battery is dead? Am I still communicating to you? No. That is because communication is both data and the energy required to convey it. How about if a friend called you to meet at a favorite restaurant and said in a happy tone, "We need to talk." That would carry a certain emotional energy that strikes your mammalian brain in a pleasant way. Yet if your boss called you into a cold, white room and said sternly, "We need to talk!" that would hit you entirely differently. The same data—the words *we need to talk*—can send two completely different messages.

This is how communications with our friends can have either a positive or negative impact on their self-esteem. In turn, that energy affects how much they value us and our standing among them. It is all in the emotional, mammalian-brain energy of the communication.

If you have had a terrible rush-hour commute home and you go out to meet friends while still carrying that negative energy, it will lower your value to them. Hopefully, you'll have already established a long track record of putting love—good energy—into them over time, consistently and mutually. This will be a buffer for you. However, if you have no track record whatsoever with a potential friend, this negative energy could mean no friendship, no deal, no job, no second date because you're sending the message that you will likely be a devaluing force in the other person's life.

We cannot control a friend's opinions. We can't force someone to change her mind no matter how many hours we shout at her, beg her, guilt-trip her, or threaten her with the loss of friendship. If anything, these actions will hasten the end of the friendship because they throw stress right into the friend's boundary. The most we can ever do in communicating with others is to have influence over them, to present a convincing idea paired with a positive

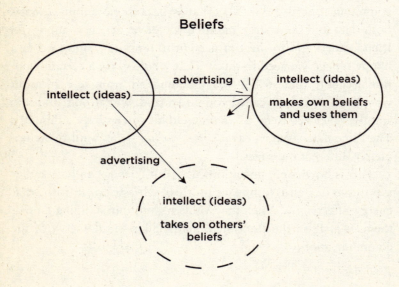

emotion that makes it even more inviting and acceptable. This is most easily done when our own boundary is strong and another's is weak and full of holes.

The very most we can do when we argue with a person whose maturity and experience is similar to our own is to *advertise*. We never control—in friendship, politics, or life in general. We can only convincingly advertise what we are and what we have to offer in value. Yet the weaker someone else's boundary is—the more immature the person is—the more easily influenced she will be. Every master marketer and snake-oil profiteer knows this. Teach people that boundaries do not exist and their belief in your brand grows while their wallet opens. Friendship is no different. I can't think of a person who has not felt like one friend or another once "sold them a bill of goods."

When we throw ideas or beliefs into the hole-ridden boundaries of friends, we are parenting them, at best, and risk abusing them at worst, turning them into robotic automatons with no original identity, authority over their lives, or responsibility for their actions. Parenting is not friendship, and it is sure to create drama, if not the eventual end of the friendship. It isn't fair to use a person far less mature than yourself just because that person has weak boundaries and is easily influenced by your ideas and beliefs.

Since we have no right to tell others how to feel, what to believe, or what to do or be, we sometimes find as we grow more intimate with friends, and temporarily open up our boundaries to each other, that there is a mismatch of beliefs. This can be fixed with a little strategy I am about to explain.

Have you ever had a friend who always had to be right, and for her to be right, you always had to be "wrong"? How did that make you feel? What did it do to your friendship? In all likelihood, it lowered the quality of your friendship and your value to each other, and things eventually went bust. Yet women's reptilian brain traps them between needing to belong and feeling bad. When you turn on your Cool Eye, you can figure it all out. You can "see" clearly, with a Seventh Sense of what people are about.

Inside our boundaries, we are all "in the right" in our own way and in accord with our beliefs. As we see in the diagram of a belief, our millions of beliefs add up to be what we call our worldview, frame of reference, or personal reality. Everyone's worldview is different. This makes our minds unique and beautiful, the source of all original art, stories, and individual paths in life. There is no such thing as absolute right or wrong in the world of mere opinion, in the world of belief.

Yet how many times per week or even per day do we get into a disagreement with friends? All the well-intentioned beginnings of teamwork together, all the months or years we spend in harmony, can be undone in one giant blowout. Opinions, you see, are never scientific facts.

Look at the diagram below and try to tell me which idea is more "in the right."

It depends on what context you are talking about: right to have an opinion or right in an absolute truth kind of way. In essence, we are all "in the right" in our own way. Our thoughts belong to us. They are located inside our boundary and what is in there is unalien-

The Communication of Opinions

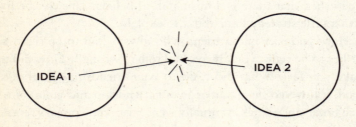

able. The only way to say that either or both of these ideas is "in the wrong" is by the force of some official, absolute truth—a fact of nature, like apples always falling down from trees rather than up. The closest thing we have to that is science, where all those who drop an apple find that it does indeed fall down, 100 percent of the time. This leads to the universal opinion we know as gravity.

In our friendships, on a day-to-day level, we will not likely have the leisure to engage in lengthy philosophical debates on metaphysics that trail deep into the night—not if we are ever to decide what movie to see together, where to dine, or what our friend ought to do about her wayward boyfriend. We will have to settle for a different tactic.

The Communication of Opinions

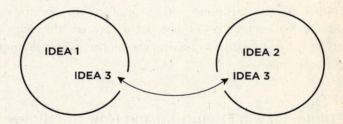

Successful communication with friends is dependent on the all-important connection I call "Idea 3." You can open up your boundary to a friend, yet still agree to disagree on the differences between your "Idea 1" and her "Idea 2." True interdependence in your friendships consists of an ability to close one of your boundary doors to things you disagree with, while simultaneously opening up another door to things you do agree with.

For all the little disagreements we have over ideas, this will work every time. The only way to get our boundary to stay open as well as that of our friend is to find an Idea 3 we both agree upon and can bond over.

If we are talking about more than just ideas, but also beliefs—ideas dearly held and locked to the floors of our minds by powerful emotions—then we have something even more powerful for bonding together in a higher quality friendship. We have access to a joint Idea 3 and to all the powerful emotion we *share* about it. In the book *The Faith Club: A Muslim, A Christian, A Jew—Three Women Search for Understanding* by Ranya Idliby, Suzanne Oliver, and Priscilla Warner, three women who suffered tremendous losses on 9/11 come to a deep understanding and connection through the Idea 3 that they cherish motherhood. This reinforces their joint and deeply held belief that the world's only answer to such tragedies is a motherly concern for those we love. Joined by what they share, their religious differences do not divide or threaten but rather educate them and, ultimately, us. These three women found the highest quality of friendship through the emotional bonds of the mammalian brain and the higher brain's mature respect for boundaries.

Diplomacy in Friendship and How the Higher Brain "Budgets" the Mammalian Brain's Emotion, Value, and Love

We can never be a perfect friend to others, but what if there was a model of perfection to shoot for—one we could never exactly achieve but which would better our lives? It would have to involve all three brains—the understanding that desire, love, and commitment are three different forces coloring friendship, love being the most common element of all friendships, the mutual, shared, positive emotion. It would recognize the basic need for people to survive and that this is not the same as true friendship, although friendship certainly aids our physical health, mental health, longevity, success, and happiness. It would see the style differences in men's and women's friendships, caused by the gender-determined instincts' influence over the higher areas of the brain. It would see that all friendships need value for both parties if they are to last. This model would take into account that we tend to like people who think the same things we think, share values and beliefs, hobbies or interests, and (not absolutely necessary, but helpful) worldviews that are similar.

It would look something like this:

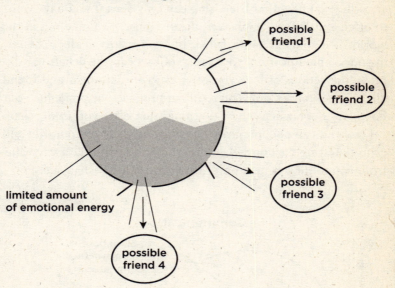

What if you were as mature in your higher brain as you could be (you had doors in your boundary instead of holes). You then went about making friends. Before you can spend your valuable resource of time or energy on others, you need to turn on your Cool Eye and look hard at your boundary. You see that there is limited energy and time but that you do have a certain amount you can spend in a discretionary way.

Friendship raises the mutual value of the two people involved—their emotional energy or happiness. Evolutionary psychologists call this a "non-zero-sum game," meaning that the value of a friendship grows far more in size than the sum of its emotional starting points. You are aware that all human beings make some constructive decisions that are win-win and some destructive ones that are win-lose. The latter is very sensible to a reptilian brain that says it is okay to live by "survival of the fittest" at the expense of others.

Still, you know that friendship can only start if you have value to offer, a little love, happiness, positive energy to send out at the world. You send out a little trickle of good energy in all directions, in your communication, your face, your words, the beliefs you express, the actions of love you offer everyone, stranger and friend alike. You put the clamps on reptilian-brain activity, opening your boundary door when others do things that offer you value, share beliefs, and can communicate constructively but temporarily and gently shutting the door when they do things that take away value from you to their benefit only, or communicate destructively.

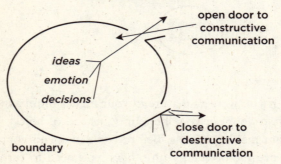

Communication

open door to
constructive
communication

ideas
emotion
decisions

close door to
destructive
communication

boundary

You notice that when you do this, it is nearly impossible to be drained by others, stressed by others, or to be used, overly influenced, or controlled by others. You feel free, happy, and you successfully reach your goals. But it is even more powerful to find friends with whom you can shoot for success. You soon notice that some of the potential friends give you good value back, you feel loved and appreciated back, communicated with, and find agreement, while others do not return much value or identification. To the latter group, you close your boundary doors tighter and start limiting any energy or time spent on them unless they drastically change their habits, boundary maturity, or constructiveness level.

You find that Friend 1 gives very little compared to what you give, so you shut the door a little on her. Friend 2 gives a fair

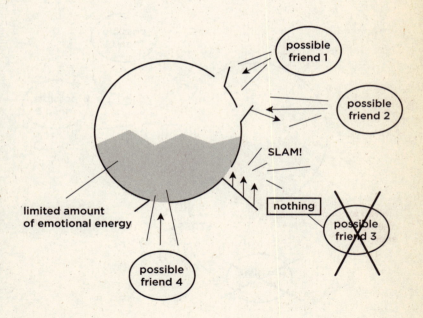

amount and you open the door wider to her. Friend 3 gives nothing at all after you gave a good amount of positive energy; you don't have time to be parent to the whole world, so you definitely close the door to immediate further contact. Friend 4 gives a massive amount in return for your small amount in the first meeting. You accept this of course and appreciate it, but will need to keep your Cool Eye turned on to see what this overly generous person is about.

Then you give a little more than before, but now to only three people.

This time Friend 1 gives back a larger amount to your larger amount of value and good energy or time. Friend 2 gives back an equal amount and is pretty consistent about it. But Friend 4

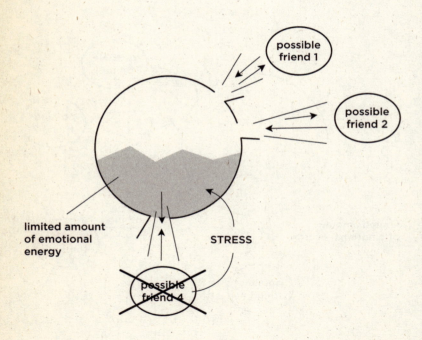

suddenly becomes very inconsistent and gives little energy back to you on the whole. In fact, she starts using you for parenting, dependently asking you to take care of her and stressing you out by trying to find other holes in you where she can dump her excess stress. You severely limit contact with this person.

You have lost very little total energy or time during all this, and in the world of physics this is called *power*, the efficient use of energy. You are seen as a good leader by the other two remaining friends and are likely to continue growing close to them. You will find that your life is easy with them and that all benefit.

This would be perfect politics among friends, using all that you now know. Perhaps one of these two will prove of such mature character and quality friendship value that you eventually consider her a best friend. But for that to happen, one other feature that combines all we know is needed, bringing together the mammalian brain and higher brain in one last way.

KWML: The Master Key to Best Friendship

Back to quantum psychology, where there are spectrums of behavior and where balance in the middle of any spectrum is the healthiest place to be. Let's say that the reptilian brain is involved in regulating our body, its safety, and the unconscious instincts and reflexes we all have, the mammalian brain is our heart, and the higher brain is our mind and will.

Since the reptilian brain is relatively uniform within each gender and people in general have a core drive to survive, there isn't much of a spectrum to it. It is fairly set in what it does for us. But we feel a wide range of mammalian-brain emotions. So, too, does intellectual skill have a wide range of expression. I showed you near the beginning of the book that character, or personality, is composed of elements of both the mammalian brain and the higher brain.

The Three Brains of a Potential Friend

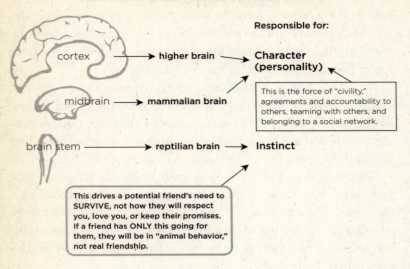

Responsible for:

cortex ———→ **higher brain** ———→ **Character (personality)**

midbrain ———→ **mammalian brain**

> This is the force of "civility," agreements and accountability to others, teaming with others, and belonging to a social network.

brain stem ————————→ **reptilian brain** ———→ **Instinct**

> This drives a potential friend's need to SURVIVE, not how they will respect you, love you, or keep their promises. If a friend has ONLY this going for them, they will be in "animal behavior," not real friendship.

We already know that self-esteem is ideally an equal mixture of well-being and confidence. A person who has every need in life—wealth, health, love, free time—but lacks the confidence to keep them is unhappy overall. A person who is supremely confident—who can fist fight, climb mountains, survive in the wild—but lacks the necessities for using that confidence to cultivate a life is also not very happy.

Being too far on either end of the spectrum of emotion is not good for us. We cannot survive physically without homeostasis (biological balance). So, too, in our psychology we need a kind of homeostasis in order to survive emotionally. This means that perfect emotional function would be at the very center of the spectrum. We call that position happiness. Nobody can have constant and perfect happiness, but we can aim for it and enjoy our growth.

In quantum psychology, imbalance is unhealthy, and people

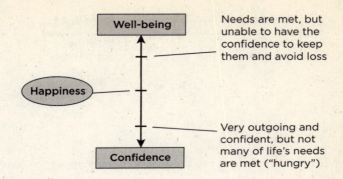

who lack either well-being relative to their level of confidence or confidence relative to their level of well-being are unhappy. When your psychological processes operate at the center of any of my spectrums, they are healthful. In the case of the well-being and confidence that compose self-esteem, the balance point is called happiness.

We need well-being the way infants need a mother, and we need confidence the way children need a father. This homeostasis, this balance, is the invisible psychology of happiness. And what of success? The psychology of success is dependent on how we use information and strategy to achieve our goals. Intellect is this skill. Still, many an intellectually brilliant Wall Street banker has been utterly miserable emotionally. And many a happy-go-lucky ne'er-do-well has lived a life of pleasure but never amounted to much success. Clearly, happiness and success do not come from the same mechanism. What if we could find happiness and success simultaneously? Friendship offers a way.

In terms of how our intellect works, being overly left-brained is akin to being obsessive-compulsive, a disorder that makes reaching personal goals very difficult for the afflicted. Obsessive-compulsive people cannot easily get out of their own heads and into action.

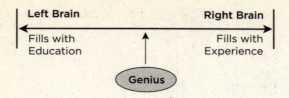

Likewise, people who are too right-brained may appear to have attention deficit disorder or, at worst, appear so disorganized they seem psychotic. The perfect place to be, intellectually, is in the center between the two, which is called *genius*. Nobody can be the ultimate genius in the world. There is always someone smarter. But we can all brush up on our intellectual skills to fill up our left brains and our experience to fill up our right brains with new learning.

If we then understand that the emotions are mammalian-brained and the intellect is higher-brained (in addition to being either more left- or more right-brained), then something interesting comes out. We are never using just one of the brains in everyday life. We are always trying to *coordinate* their use, though we are usually a bit out of balance. We are not just "heart," and not just "mind." We are both.

If we cross these two spectrums, it shows us all the possible ways that we coordinate our mammalian brains and higher brains at the same time. All possible functions of personality can be represented as being in one of these four quadrants.

We are all either more full of confidence or more full of well-being at any given time. We are more analytical and orderly (left-brained), more reliant on our education and lessons past to make sense of the world, or more disorganized, wild, and creative intellectually—more reliant on our experience to chart a future.

The Cognitive-emotional Spectrums
Defining All Human Behavior

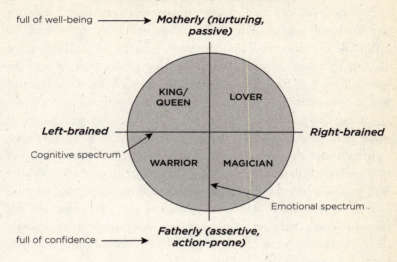

full of well-being ———→ *Motherly (nurturing, passive)*

Left-brained ——— *Right-brained*

Cognitive spectrum

KING/QUEEN   LOVER

WARRIOR   MAGICIAN

Emotional spectrum

full of confidence ———→ *Fatherly (assertive, action-prone)*

The main point of anything called quantum is that something can be both a particle and a wave at the same time, can have both a certainty of position and a probability of being located in a general region of space. In psychology, this means we can both function in a certain way right now and favor a certain style of personality or level of character. In this graph, we move higher in maturity of personality, and therefore character, as we slowly, solidly find ourselves positioned closer and closer to the center of the circle, where balance is.

Have you ever noticed yourself calling a friend "out of whack," "imbalanced," "off," or another name that generally means that person is a little extreme in personality? Maybe this irked you or maybe you thought it was quaint. Either way, in scientific terms what you were saying is that the person's personality or character was generally functioning somewhere at the outskirts of the circle above.

Since we have two spectrums that cut each other into quadrants, a quantum psychology would tell us that anybody can be anything in their behavior at a given moment: we could be ordinarily shy but one day break out into song and laughter with friends; we could be ordinarily out of control and impulsively angry, yet suddenly calm and caring when we notice our sister's new child carried into the room. Yet we all have a general favored area of this circle that we like to operate within. It is our most probable place to be.

I label these King or Queen, Warrior, Magician, and Lover in my system, and the names make symbolic sense. Much has been written about these four particular names in literature on men's studies and medieval history, but I use them as general good descriptors of the style of personality in both men and women, and with a special set of diagrams, rules, and dynamics that are not found in other literature. I suggest that we grow from an original temperament we were born into genetically toward fuller maturity by gaining skills in the other three we lack.

A person with a King temperament is a male who is nurturing and motherly to people—in other words, full of well-being in his mammalian brain. In his higher brain, he uses a logical, analytical, detail-oriented way of processing information. Many call this being *left-brained*. A Queen is a woman with the same style.

A Warrior, whether male or female, is also a person who is left-brained or analytical, yet has a mammalian brain more dominant in the type of self-esteem we have called confidence. Emotionally, others may notice that whether a man or a woman, Warriors have a fatherly presence, pushing others to face risks, changes in life, or losses with just as much fortitude as they possess themselves. They are quick to assess data very concretely and to jump into targeted action.

A Magician is simply a person who is also an action taker, more confident and fatherly in her mammalian brain than she is nurturing, motherly, or full of the well-being that draws her to meet the needs of others. Yet in her higher brain, she processes data in very creative, visionary ways—a cognitive style some have termed *right-brained*. These people love to entertain an audience but are loath to give each audience member one-on-one advice.

Finally, the Lover style of personality temperament is someone also right-brained or artistic, like the Magician, but dominated emotionally in the mammalian brain by an abundance of well-being. This makes Lovers emotionally nurturing like the Kings or Queens but intellectually more creative and less detail oriented.

The graph of these four types of personality shows us that opposites—Kings/Queens with Magicians, or Lovers with Warriors—provide each other perfect emotional and intellectual support simply by being who they are. This is the stuff of best friendship—not a labor, but an energizing, intellectually stimulating connection that is so strong, it is likely to last for life.

What this means for your friendships is that the type of personality you associate with matters greatly if you find yourself devoting a lot of resources, intimacy, and time to them. Who you befriend matters not only in terms of having shared higher-brain beliefs, values, interests, and maturity level, but also in terms of how you *complement* each other or work together as a team of friends who both want success and happiness out of your connection. Like attracts like in the higher brain's beliefs, values, and intellectual goals. We like people who share the same political, religious, and social worldviews. Yet in our personality styles, *opposites* attract because of how such opposites complete what we lack in emotional and intellectual skills. Our opposites in personality style make our friendship a perfect, well-rounded team to tackle the shared goals of life.

When you are in friendship with a Queen-style person and you are a Queen yourself, you do not offer each other anything new in value. Eventually, you are going to be in conflict or competition because of your reptilian brain's need to belong or, for males, to have rank over those around you. The same goes for Warriors, Magicians, and Lovers.

If you are a Lover and are friends with a Magician, you have a great complementarity of emotional energy: you are full of well-being and she is full of confidence. Together, as a team of friends, you have complete self-esteem, though you may both be a little over the top in terms of disorganized overly artistic thinking. If you are a Warrior with a Magician friend, you both have a great complementarity of intellect and can solve many problems together to team up for success, yet you lack an emotional bond where you have something to offer that the other does not. The same would be true of a Queen and a Lover friendship.

The perfect pairing of personality styles or characters is to have a friend who is opposite yourself in both emotional energy and intellectual style. Kings or Queens pair as best friends with Magicians, and Lovers and Warriors pair as best friends. Why? They bring to the table exactly what the other lacks naturally.

In KWML we don't see people as stationary, stuck in a certain temperament for life—as does the Myers-Briggs Type Indicator measures you may have taken at work or the typical online dating quizzes. I think you'll find it far more useful than other measures, and you can test yourself and potential best friends and lovers in the free quiz at www.womenshappiness.com.

Whatever you assess yourself (and others) to be, you'll find friendship far smoother with those who are your opposite, as long as you have cultivated mature boundaries, have a working knowledge of the reptilian brain, and understand the equations and diagrams that lay out the perfect system for diagnosing and treating your friendship problems. If character is destiny, yours will grow and become rich with success and happiness as you follow the stories to come and apply them to the stories of your own friendships from now on.

PART TWO

Putting the Psychology of Friendship to Work

Chapter Five

Friends in Need

It is not so much our friends' help that helps us as the confident knowledge they will help us.

—Epicurus

Sue felt *as though she were walking through Jell-O. In the hour since she'd returned from the hospital, she could barely make sense of anything. Relatives moved around her, but it was as though they were in some other universe entirely, a universe where Sue could see them but not feel them in any way. Sue knew her mother had been dying; she was horribly sick for more than a year. Still, that didn't make the reality of her death any easier to accept. Sue knew she'd have the feeling of that last touch of her mother's hand in her heart for the rest of her life.*

The sense of thickness in the air embraced Sue so completely that she barely noticed when the doorbell rang. She told herself she should answer it, but her body failed to follow the command. Instead, she continued to try to make the turkey sandwich for Aunt Jess that she'd been trying to make for the past ten minutes.

"I came as soon as I heard."

Sue recognized the voice, but it didn't register at first. Only when Kate wrapped her arms around her did Sue realize that her friend was here. She was more than a little surprised to find Kate in the kitchen with her. In fact, she wasn't even sure how Kate knew what was going on.

Kate's embrace lasted so long that it began to feel uncomfortable, especially since Sue's arms were pinned to her sides. Eventually, she got them free and hugged Kate back. Only then did Kate loosen up, stepping back and taking Sue's head in her hands.

"You must be horribly sad," Kate said.

Sue's eyes brimmed. "I miss her so much."

Kate hugged her again and then took her hand. "Come on, let's go."

Sue noticed some of her other relatives looking at her. Few of them knew Kate, and they were probably wondering what this person was doing here during a time of family grief. "Go where?"

"Someplace quiet. There are so many people here. Do your parents have a guest room?"

Sue gestured with her head. "It's down the hall."

Kate pulled on her hand. "Let's go there and talk."

"I really should be here right now. Some people are still on their way."

Kate glanced at the others. If she noticed that they looked at her as an "outsider," she didn't give any indication of it. "You need a break from this. Come on."

Still feeling as though she was out of sync with the rest of the world, Sue followed Kate to the tiny guest bedroom next to the den. They sat on the bed facing each other and Kate said, "Tell me everything you're feeling."

As dulled as Sue felt, she allowed herself a little inward chuckle. This was classic Kate. How many times had they sat together with other friends while Kate played armchair therapist to the group? Sue wondered why Kate never finished her degree in psychology, choosing to become a paralegal instead. Maybe she figured this gave her two occupations—one she could use at work and another she could trot out whenever the crowd got together.

Kate had a unique way of approaching any problem a friend might be having. She'd ask probing questions—sometimes a little too probing for in public—and then develop some life lesson based on her own experience. Sue remembered the time she had a drink with Kate after Brad broke up with her. Kate pulled all kinds of stuff out of her, including things she'd never told anyone else about her love life. Sue had had this kind of experience with Kate before, and it always made her feel a little uneasy. Yet when Kate started sharing intensely intimate details about her own love losses to give Sue some perspective, Sue felt at least a little consoled. Eventually, she even found herself propping Kate up that night, helping her to overcome regrets over an ex-boyfriend who'd done her wrong.

"I'm not sure what I'm feeling right now," Sue said as they sat on the bed.

"Don't hide from it, Sue. Let it out. You know you need to."

Sue felt her lips quiver. "She was my rock. Even when she was so sick. I don't know what I'll do without her."

Kate took her hand and patted it. "I know what you're feeling, and I'm here for you. Do you feel that there were unresolved things between the two of you?"

Sue shook her head slowly. "No, I really don't. We had some beautiful conversations toward the end." She paused to let a wave of sadness pass. "I just wish I could have more of them."

Over the next several minutes, Sue shared the details of some of those conversations while Kate offered advice and reflection through her own stories. Sue already knew from several late-night talks that Kate had a very different relationship with her mother than Sue had with hers. Kate's parents divorced when she was a child, and it was obvious that had left some scars. In fact, it was a rare night when the conversation didn't veer to the divorce at some point.

"I was making a sandwich a little while ago," Sue said mournfully, "and I thought about this chutney my mother sometimes put on sandwiches. My first thought was to ask her where she got *it . . . and then I realized that I could never ask questions like that again."*

"It's tough, Sue, I know. Believe me, I really know. Getting over the loss of a loved one is incredibly difficult, even when you've had some time to prepare. I mean, I knew instinctively that my parents were going to split up because of all of the fighting. But when it actually happened, I was devastated."

Kate wiped her eyes and Sue felt a little twinge of sympathy. "I know all about death in the family," Kate continued. "My parents' divorce was just like a death—the death of what could have been a perfect household."

Tears now rolled down Kate's cheeks. Sue felt the urge to comfort her.

And then she drew herself up short. Through the haze of her grief, Sue suddenly saw something with crystal clarity—Kate had come here under the guise of supporting her but she was really seeking support instead. Now that she thought about it, Sue realized that Kate's "counseling sessions" always turned out this way. She was endlessly needy.

Abruptly, Sue stood up from the bed. "You need to go now."

Kate sniffled. "No. I'm going to be here for you."

"You're not here for me, Kate. You're here for you. Please leave."

Kate seemed baffled, but she slowly stood up and headed toward the door. Before she left, she turned back and said, "This is no way to treat a friend."

Sue decided not to respond. She knew this was exactly how to treat this friend.

What Psyche Has to Say about Neediness

Oh, neediness. It gives us a creepy feeling and at the same time often pulls at our heartstrings. Regardless, neediness comes with risks—of lost resources in terms of your time, energy, freedom, and even money.

One can read the myth of Psyche as an allegory that speaks to the challenge of maturely navigating through the needy friendships of our lives. The maturely feminine Aphrodite charged the girlish Psyche with three impossible tasks in order to get her husband back from her. First, Psyche had to sort a million red seeds from white ones. Fortunately, a million little ants came along to assist her, naturally doing the sorting themselves. Then Psyche needed to steal the exquisite fur of a herd of wild boars that could surely kill her. Psyche found that marsh reeds naturally catch the hair from the beasts as they pass, and she collected it at night. Finally, she had to obtain a goblet of water from the river Styx. The eagle of Zeus came to her aid, swooping down to grab the goblet, dip it in the water, and deliver it to her hands.

The parallels to the lives of all women are abundant here. We see that as a woman grows spiritually she will have to face the test of seeds: to learn to sort things out (using her boundary ability to reach goals through patience and persistence). She will face the need to deal with conflict and danger, with triadic relationships that aren't necessarily smooth or easy. So she learns to organically, naturally, allow people's character to declare their destiny, to pass the test of the boars' hair (allowing the natural course of things to alleviate the greatest dangers). Finally, she learns that in the adult life of mature character she will need to dip into the creativity of the unconscious, to solve problems she is grieving over, pondering, or processing bit by bit, and accept good help when it is available.

After all three of these tests, Aphrodite sends Psyche on a long heroic journey down into the underworld. With her she is to take two coins (to pay the boatman Charon, there and back), and two bean cakes (to distract the three-headed dog Cerberus, the hound of hell, there and back). On the way, she is tempted by the desperate and needy—an old lady who begs for a coin to pay Charon for passage and an old man who is hungry and asks for a bean cake. Psyche faces her girlish instincts to share, to give to the needy, and enjoy the temporary importance of being valued by desperate others. But she also realizes that if she gives the woman a coin, she will not be able to return to the world of the living with the rewards of feminine maturity. If she gives the man a cake, she will not be able to pass by the three-headed guard dog of the underworld to complete her heroic journey to adulthood and lasting marriage to Eros.

This is one of the hardest lessons for women to learn about developing friendship skills, for it is against core feminine nature to withhold support when friends ask for it or to deny friends a sense of belonging. Yet if one profound goal of women is to reach the rewards of maturity, there will come a time when she will have to learn to turn away the needy to provide for herself. Her boundary may be full of enough self-esteem to give and give and give energy away in friendship, but if she does too much of this, she will eventually feel overwhelmed by the stress of the needy friends in her life.

Beyond reptilian-brain instinct, other things encourage women to give to needy friends. Sometimes it is a desire to be important in the minds of others through giving. Sometimes it is an avoidance of guilt. Sometimes it is an echo of other experiences: a guilt-tripping mom, a wish to feel important in a weak father's eyes, a codependent marriage. When we are young, adults bond to us when we are overly agreeable, always saying yes to their requests. But in the adult world we get far more respect for our boundaries by saying no.

This is not to say that we ought to deny needy friends at all times. Helping others is part of the joy of friendship, bonding, and belonging. But you need to do this when you are full of resources, using your boundary with doors, not holes, and with discrimina-

Needy Friend

Abundant Friend

tion, not willy-nilly. There are friends who are needy and others who are abundant (though this is always a relative thing).

How to Be a Supportive but Mature Friend

Your boundary is an immensely powerful thing about you. It provides a means of "knowing yourself" and shaping an identity by virtue of having preferences in every area of your life. It also offers you a means of helping others know who you are, what you prefer, where your limits are, and what exactly you offer in friendship and on what terms.

When you do not use your boundary with others and let them lean too heavily and too often on you, your friendships tend to be a source of depletion of your good energy and time. In the short run, this might make you feel proud of yourself for being a good friend who "goes the extra mile" for your buddies. However, in the long run you tend to deplete yourself entirely and become the

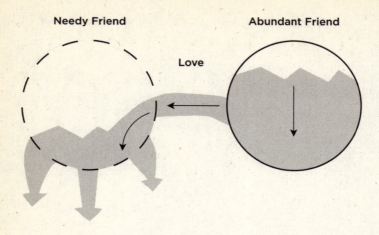

worst friend ever, crashing completely and unable to give even the smallest amount to others.

When you continue to give love to a friend who does not or will not grow better boundaries (with doors instead of walls), you will eventually deplete your own energy through that friend's weak boundary. This will happen even if you have reasonable strength and solidity.

Going the extra distance to support others is hardwired into the feminine reptilian brain. But as Psyche learned from Aphrodite, this is not the path to mature womanhood and feminine accomplishment. Bonding and giving in extremes to those we are bonded to is a feminine instinct evolved for the purpose of protection of our children. If you have your Cool Eye turned on, though, you'll notice that even adult friends are rarely the exact same age on the inside. Constantly needy friends tend to be childlike in their *psychological age* (what psychoanalysts call "developmental level"). Aphrodite taught Psyche that she did not agree to be mother to the entire world. Adult friendships are not for parenting others or being their ever-available, all-knowing therapists. They are, as the master checklist indicates, for *mutual* growth.

Go back to Sue from the story at the beginning of this chapter. Sue realized, at a time when she was terribly vulnerable herself, that Kate was draining her with her neediness. Sue did what she needed to do—and what Kate needed her to do as well, though Kate couldn't admit it in the moment. She announced to Kate that she would no longer be a party to her neediness.

When you use an adult boundary on needy friends there are several things you can do to be mature and still honor your feminine side. For one, when you say no to a friend because you just do not have the resources to share, this is far better than trying to give to others what you don't have to give. In essence, this is like offering a needy friend a million-dollar check and then announcing that it is likely to bounce. This action is not friendly, honest, or empathetic. It is childish, even though it might make you feel like you are important and caring.

Think of the instructions they give us at the beginning of airline flights. They tell us that if cabin pressure drops, we should put on our own oxygen masks before even helping our children. They don't say this because they want us to be selfish. They say this because they know we need to be strong (have enough oxygen) before we can help others effectively. The same is true of our relations with needy friends.

If you clearly see that your friend in need can solve some of her own problems with patience, it is okay to say no to her requests for your energy or time. When you do this, you can avoid being depleted by her and you can show her that she has it in her to be successful and happy. It is just a matter of telling her that her boundary can be fixed by getting better at tolerating and hearing the word *no*. Doing this makes you more trustworthy as a friend rather than less so. You will be seen as honest and reliable enough to show your friend what's real about life: that as adults we need

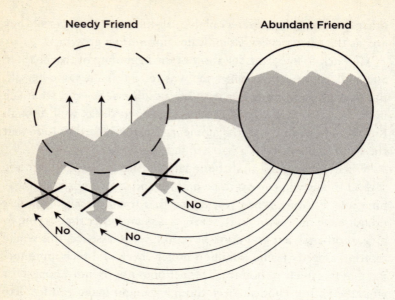

Needy Friend   **Abundant Friend**

to learn to solve problems we can handle with autonomy and personal accountability and responsibility.

In fact, the personal boundary is the precise aspect of our psyches that allows us to budget our resources and even our money. As children, we had no choice over whether we came from a well-to-do family or a poverty-stricken one. But as adults, we are expected by society to develop a boundary with doors in it, where we are personally responsible for budgeting money, energy, and everything else. So, in effect, in the adult world it is our fault when we are psychologically needy. When we explain this to needy friends, they may not like hearing it, but they will ultimately come around to thank you for having made them a better person through tough love.

When you use tough love with a friend, you are saying no to her for her good and your good. This helps to patch the holes in her boundary. Once you do this for her, she can then work at building up her own internal self-esteem rather than always borrowing yours. The way we already learned to build our own self-esteem is through using *assertiveness* (in the Anger Map) and *courage* (in the Anxiety Map).

The way to manage the balance between being true to both your femininity and your destiny in adulthood is to recognize that it isn't your job to be either a storehouse or a charm school for friends. In addition, remember, with your Cool Eye turned on, that "it takes a village to raise a child." Keep in mind that women tend to support each other better in social networks. Get your whole circle of friends involved when a friend is frequently needy.

How to Avoid Being a Needy Friend

If you yourself were occasionally needy, it would feel right and normal to go to good friends for some support. But if your friends consider you frequently needy, chances are you would not be aware of this opinion. You would not even know you were "the needy friend." Why? Because when we have holes in our boundaries, we can't see them until we master the use of our Cool Eye.

Kate in the story that opened this chapter had no idea that she had some considerable boundary holes and was therefore always in need. She believed she was helping her friends, but in fact, her "counseling sessions" always became about *her* issues. Kate's trouble was that she had unresolved grief about her parents' divorce. She turned this into a drive to help others and this gave her a greater sense of value. But then her boundary holes caused her to project her troubles onto others (even while she was supposed to be helping them), and this made her friends feel as though she was much too needy and to grow tired of her act.

One of the first steps to detecting friendship neediness in your-self, and fixing it, is to have your Cool Eye turned on. Interacting with friends is the only way for adults to find out where their bound-ary holes are. Notice when friends give you feedback, whether in word or in behavior, and value that feedback.

If you find that friends roll their eyes at you when you com-plain yet again about how much you hate your job, don't see them as insensitive. Process it in your head. Use your Cool Eye to ask yourself questions about how you are doing socially. Why would they roll their eyes? Could it be that if you don't like your job, you should stop complaining and do something about it? If your friends tell you after two years of your fretting over the boyfriend who broke up with you that they are "tired of hearing about it," could it be that they literally mean it? When we fret, complain, or "dump" on others, we are failing to follow the master friendship checklist because we are being neither *mutual* nor *positive*. We are dumping the negative energy called anxiety into our friends' boundaries. We win; they lose.

Your Cool Eye, followed by some work on your boundary, helps you shed the "needy" label. If you can see what was invisible before, you have a Seventh Sense of people and of yourself. You will see that you have negative energy in you, that you often dump it on others, and that while that feels good, it is lowering the quality and number of your friendships. In the long run this is not good for you.

So when your friends give you feedback that makes you feel surprised or uncomfortable about what they think of you, it is not the time to make up excuses or avoid looking at what they mean. It is a time for *courage*. Have the courage to look at yourself, and realize that friends are not a threat; they are helping you grow as a village raises a child. They are showing you your boundary holes. If we were to continue the story of Kate and Sue, the best outcome would be that Kate would learn from Sue's "dismissal" that she was doing something to drive friends away and would ultimately learn how to stop doing this.

To fix neediness, we need to find the courage to be self-sufficient and the ability to hear the word no with grace and acceptance. Here is a paradigm shift for you. Although it goes against your passionate feminine need for acceptance, consider that rejection makes you grow. That's right: if you were to try welcoming rejection from others, you would be open to learning where your boundary holes are. This is not to say that you should purposely try to offend or get cast out from your circles of friends. Be yourself, but in the times when people happen to reject you, see that as a gift, a boundary hole through which you didn't even know you were dumping bad energy.

The master checklist is useful through all aspects of being a friend. We have looked at how the problem of neediness in friendships lacks mutuality. If you or your friend are needy *once in a while*, then helping each other reaffirms your natural, reptilian-brain femininity through belonging and supporting each other's *security*. However, if you or your friend are frequently or often unexpectedly needy, the relationship overall is not mutual; it is a one-sided, unfair, destructive deal for at least one of you.

The notion of being consistently needy is not an advantage in friendship. *Consistency* in friendship needs to be the kind that amplifies good emotion between you. If, when you feel needy, you were to consistently strive for solutions to your problems and autonomy over them (rather than running on a treadmill of negativity and lack of self-responsibility), you would build your relationships. Seeing this makes your supportive friend feel good even though you feel bad. She can see with her Cool Eye that you will feel better in the future thanks to her support.

Likewise, if you are supporting a needy friend you can help the friendship by being consistently on message with your belief that your friend can and will learn to solve her problems for herself. If you are consistent in your tough love—bringing both your empathy and your willingness to point out tough realities—this builds friendship.

While males may handle needy friendships simply by avoiding them, women have that special reptilian-brain challenge of feeling that avoiding a frequently needy friend is "not right." The master checklist includes the need for *sharing* for any relationship to truly be called a friendship. In your needy friendship, you will have and want to continue sharing feelings and ideas with each other, but this does not mean that you have to have lots of holes in your boundary in the ways you connect. You can both share and recognize that your friend's problems are theirs, not yours.

Someone who is needy is low in self-esteem at that moment. You may have so much abundance in you that at first you simply give your good energy away. As we learned, making a codependent habit of this only leads to all of your good efforts and resources draining out the holes in the bottom of your friend's boundary. Once you use good boundaries with your needy friend, your next, most efficient step is to show her exactly how to use the Anger and Anxiety maps. This mentoring shows her how to convert her own negative energy (which stresses you) into positive energy and high self-esteem—the well-being that comes from her getting her own needs met and the confidence that comes from facing her own fears to find very personal solutions.

Chapter Six

Juggling Friendships

Sir, I look upon every day to be lost, in which I do not make a new acquaintance.

—SAMUEL JOHNSON

LORI STARED *at the telephone. She couldn't remember the last time she'd been so stymied about making a call. What was especially confounding was that the call she needed to make was to one of her dearest friends in the world.*

What am I afraid of? *Lori wondered.* Cathy's always understood me. She's always supported me. Nothing's changed. Nothing at all.

Lori knew she was kidding herself. Quite a bit had changed. In some ways, everything was different now. She and Cathy had become best friends when they were nurses in the same hospital, making the long hours of work zip away and spending endless amounts of time at play having a great time and connecting at a level that bordered on sisterly (actually, Lori liked Cathy a whole lot more than she liked her sister). They'd shared dating war stories, turning heartbreak into hilarity, and double-dated on numerous occasions.

Then Cathy met Rick. One look at Cathy's face as she talked about him told Lori that Rick was a serious keeper. And when she saw the way Cathy and Rick were together, she knew that Cathy's single days would soon be over. Within eighteen months, there was a wedding and a baby—and the dilemma that now had Lori staring at the phone as though it were going to bite her.

How could the christening be on the same day as the Vail event? Who did I tick off to have such rotten luck?

When Lori got the invitation to little Emily's christening, she couldn't wait to go. She'd only seen the baby in person once, and the pictures Cathy e-mailed her regularly made Emily look like the cutest kid ever born. She couldn't wait to snuggle her "niece" in her arms. But the next day, some other friends told her about the biggest singles event of the summer up in Vail. Every gorgeous single man was going to be there—and gorgeous single men had a very special place in Lori's heart.

For the past two days, Lori struggled to make a decision about where to go. She was in a very lonely place in life. Vail would be very good for her. But if she let Cathy down, what kind of friend would she be? Lori had had problems juggling friendships in the past. She'd even seen a therapist about it when things got too stressful. The therapist had some good advice, but none of it seemed to apply to leaving your closest friend out in the cold. Still, she couldn't miss the event in Vail. If she did, she might regret it forever.

At last, she made her decision. She had to choose Vail over the christening and hope Cathy would understand. Now she just had to pick up the phone that stared back at her venomously.

Deal with it, girl. You owe Cathy that much.

Lori screwed up her courage and hit number two on the speed dial. Cathy answered on the second ring.

"Hey, I was just thinking about you," Cathy said brightly.

Lori squeezed her eyes shut. Great. This is going to be even worse than I thought. "Listen, I need to talk to you about the christening."

"Oh, it's gonna be fantastic! That Italian place you love is catering it."

Lori cringed. "Do you think I can get a doggie bag?"

"Huh?"

Lori tried to get all of the words out at once. "You're gonna hate me, but the Vail Blowout is the same weekend and—"

"The Vail Blowout."

Lori continued to speak quickly. "You know what they say about the guys there and everything and—"

Cathy's laughter exploded in Lori's ear. "Are you telling me you actually considered coming to my cozy little baby party instead of going to the greatest guy fest on three continents?"

Cathy's response so startled Lori that she couldn't speak.

"Lori, you didn't think I'd be mad about this, did you?"

"I kinda did, actually."

"Let me tell you something," Cathy said, still chuckling. "I love you dearly, you know that, and I would love to have you here. But between the baby, my relatives, and a bunch of other people who are coming, I'll survive. You, on the other hand, must go to Vail."

Lori felt a warm rush of relief wash over her. "I'm so glad you feel that way."

Cathy laughed again. "You are going to owe me something when you return, though."

"I already have a great present for the baby."

"Yes, that's what I was thinking—that you owed me a present for the baby. I'm not talking about a present. I'm talking about details!"

Lori let out her own boisterous laugh. "You got it."

Learning to Juggle with Your Three Brains

We have several parts of our psychology to consider when we think about juggling friendships. First, juggling involves good skill with our personal boundaries—the very thing that lets us budget time and energy. Second, we spend the most time with people with whom we have the most in common. We learned earlier that the whole concept of "liking" comes about not just from the good emotions we feel in the presence of others but in the similarity these people have to ourselves. Finally, the feminine instinct toward connection, belonging, and harmony takes hold.

The story of Lori and Cathy illustrates all of this. Lori had a great deal of work to do on her boundaries, including learning to put herself first and to "fill up" on internal resources before giving those away to others. A more vibrant romantic life as a single was certainly one of those things. Lori and Cathy also had a great deal in common even though Cathy is married with a child. They are both nurses and worked together for a number of years, sharing experiences socially and professionally. They have a lengthy and rich *history* together. Projecting forward, we would find Lori has learned to have more faith in the harmonious workings of the feminine instinct and its tendency to seek harmony and shared compromise, finding Cathy a welcoming, loyal friend who knew her enough and had good-enough boundaries to recognize Lori's need for self-care.

Understanding how to juggle friendships requires a look at the three brains.

The Higher Brain's Juggling Ability

Our personal boundary lets us know what we prefer and what we don't, what is good for us and what is not, and what is our responsibility and what is someone else's. Cathy's happiness with the birth of her baby is Cathy's responsibility, not Lori's. Likewise, Lori's pleasure or displeasure with her own romantic life is Lori's responsibility, not Cathy's. Many women find that, while the nature of their friendships change when one gets married, this does not have to be the end of the world. In fact, friendships between marrieds and singles can actually be enriching for both. Marrieds can find a link to excitement, bonding, and freedom through their single friends, often living vicariously through them and feeding a sexual fantasy life by proxy that they can then bring back to the secure confines of their marriage. Likewise, singles can find a link to safety and feeling "grounded" when romantic drama creeps into their lives, and they can glimpse a future where they might also be married.

Perhaps the greatest change in this situation, however, is the amount of time friends have to share together. Both our boundary and our master checklist help with this.

Your boundary helps you manage time as much as it helps you manage emotional energy, and the prospect of juggling friendships necessitates that you learn to manage time well. In *Poor Richard's Almanack*, Benjamin Franklin described "a perfect day" as, "Eight hours of work, eight hours of play, and eight hours of rest." We can look at it this way:

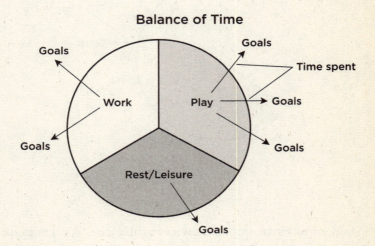

Balance of Time

When we set goals of friendship or even meet ups with our friends that fit with the three areas of our lives, we will find a healthy balance in which we get both our own needs met and consistent quality time with friends for mutual enjoyment, sharing, and the fun of happy emotion together. Imagine having six days in your week, with one in your pocket for unforeseen needs. Some of those days could be spent with a friend working on a project you enjoy together, some of the others can be dedicated to a playful, fun activity like taking in some music or dinner together, and the rest can be used for doing something healthful, restful, or rejuvenating like exercise, going to the spa, or shopping for health foods. Your boundary is fundamental to this because it lets you say no to some things in your week and yes to others.

Unfortunately, most of us arrange what could have been a perfect day more like this:

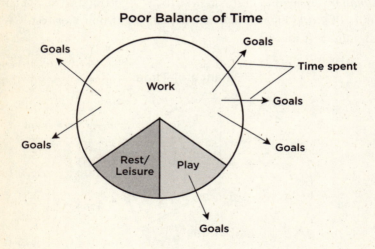

Poor Balance of Time

Many of us let work dominate everything else of value in our lives. Sometimes this is out of fear of not having enough money or greed at wanting to buy the next toy or afford that vacation. If we find ourselves suffering for friendship, though, we come to the realization that there is no higher value in life than a friend. The best jobs come on the recommendation of friends, the best dates with the opposite sex on referral from them, the most secure identity from them. They even give us a couch to crash on when we lose our jobs or our soul mates.

You can even make a diagram of your ideal balance on a big piece of paper. Perhaps you'd rather diagram a week instead of a day, and perhaps you want to subdivide rest, work, and play into all the dearest areas of life.

Example of the Perfect Week

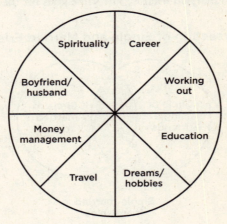

Another function of the higher brain that Lori could have used sooner is what we know as "liking." Our common interests are a way of joining our personal needs with the need to cultivate friendships—once again with consistent, mutual, shared positive emotion.

Part of having good boundaries is understanding that we aren't responsible for the budgeting of our friends' time. It is okay when they say no, just as it is okay when we say no to a chance to meet up. What Lori didn't see as obvious was that Cathy had a very fulfilling marriage and immediate family who were going to be there to share in the joy of the christening. Lori wasn't taking that much away from the celebration by not being there. However, if she'd shown up resentful, impatient, or trying to double-book the christening along with her singles event, she may have generated negative emotion. It really was the best move to treat herself well first and then worry about finding another time to meet Cathy.

For single people, having a rich variety of other single friends with common interests is a good foundation from which to have even more to give to married friends. The same goes for the marrieds.

Intersection of Single and Married Friends

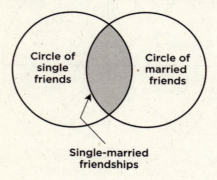

Single-married
friendships

When thinking about juggling schedules, remember that what is important is whether, over the long haul, both friends have a general experience of positive emotion, and have an ongoing source of it from both inside (through assertiveness and courage) and outside themselves (from circles of friends). If the single friend is sorely lacking in a social network of other singles, she won't make a very good friend to the married person and if the married friend has a terrible marriage full of negative drama, she too will not be a very good friend to the single person. If you and your friends have balance and respect for each others' time via your boundaries, though, you can navigate even the stickiest of friendship juggling problems.

The Mammalian Brain and Juggling Friendships

It's all about positive emotion, remember. So it is important that the mammalian brain concentrate on ways of cultivating opportunity for personal assertiveness, courage, and belonging to a number of circles of friends. We all need to wrestle with issues of jealousy, depression, fear, and other negative emotions, converting them to positives if we are to remain true to our master checklist.

When we fail to manage the emotional side of juggling friendships well, one of the biggest issues to come up is jealousy. It is important to remember that when we say yes to what lowers our good energy, it hurts everyone. Even when we say no to what doesn't work for our schedules, it may give rise to jealousy in our temporarily rejected friend. She might think, "Does this mean I'm not important? Does this mean I can't count on her when I really need her?"

We know jealousy is a negative emotion. Next, we need to assess whether it is more on the anger end or anxiety end of the spectrum. For most people, jealousy is an angry emotion. To be on the receiving end of it is a negative experience and one that tears down friendships quickly. Many women are not aware of how destructive their jealousy is to others and therefore to their friendships. It is easy to be alone inside our heads when we are jealous, but remember, as in most experiences in friendship, everything that happens affects not only one but both people. The Anger Map is your key to fixing this problem, and we will cover jealousy extensively in the next chapter.

The Reptilian Brain and Juggling Relationships

A woman's natural, passionate need to belong is the very thing that drives her to expand her social network, even if this occasionally leads her to being overcommitted.

Once again, your degree of belonging may play out in multiple circles of friends, and yet you can juggle them all with the natural feminine tendency to make introductions: to harmonize and join various circles of friends.

If you were to hide or keep your circles of friends separate and distinct (as the male reptilian brain tends to do), you present yourself with extra energy expenditure in maintaining these separate relationships. You may spend a great deal of time trying to coor-

Friendship Triangles and Circles of Friends

Circle of friends 1

Circle of friends 3   Circle of friends 2

dinate between the various differing plans of the groups just to be able to belong to them all. You may find your plate too full and your heart too stressed by the needs and values of three separate groups sailing off in different directions, with you caught and pulled at the center.

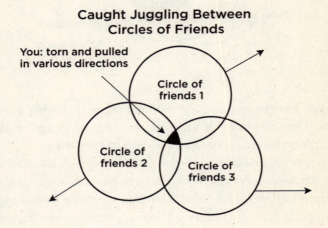

Caught Juggling Between Circles of Friends

This is not a good situation for you to try to maintain for great lengths of time. Fortunately, you can use the natural gifts of the feminine reptilian brain here: you can find the points where all your circles of friends join and, whenever you get the chance, introduce members from the various groups.

Notice how the arrows of different direction are much smaller when three circles of friends have been joined better. The pressure on you as the *introducer* is much less, and, instead of breaking promises to all three groups (showing them what a low-quality friend you are through poor boundaries), you actually find you are most highly valued and sense even more belonging than you could have in any one group alone. People recognize you as the reason

Joining Circles of Friends

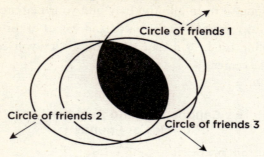

they now have more positive emotional energy than they ever had before. They connect this great emotion to the image of you in their minds and remember to invite you to everything.

When women make circles of friends expand, their reptilian brains are satisfied because there is even more intimacy and good energy to tap into. This feeds a woman's instinct for safety, harmony, and balance. In times of drama or challenge, she has a much greater network to tap into and has done so without sending her energy and time in conflicting directions.

Sometimes we have friends who are going through changes of life that move them toward a very different set of interests and priorities from our own. When this happens, don't fret. You may find, as Lori did, that you can spend a great deal of your time with the circles with whom you have the most in common but still stay strongly connected to the friends who don't belong as much. When she couldn't physically visit as often, Lori's e-mail, texting, and phone calls meant the world to Cathy in terms of Lori's consistency, and they produced good emotion even when the friends couldn't share in person as often once the baby came.

The Juggling Checklist

- Do I have a budget diagram that shows balance in how I spend my time with friends in work, play, and leisure activities?

- Do I maintain consistent communication with my friends even if I spend a different amount of time and energy on each?

- Do all my friends know where my needs and boundaries lie?

- Do they know what we have in common and make efforts at compromise so that we can both enjoy our time together?

- Do I have my Cool Eye turned on enough to know when I am stretched too thin or when I am tending to say yes to more than I can realistically keep promises about?

- How many circles of friends do I have and what opportunities do I have to join some of them?

- Do I feel a sense of loyalty to and from my friends? Which ones? If not, can I communicate boundaries better to understand where their time needs and mine could be more harmoniously joined in a shared activity?

- Do I have a sense of belonging in most of my circles of friends? Do I need to join some or leave some for a while to correct this balance?

- Do I make my friends feel a sense of belonging by doing my share of inviting them to join *my* circles or feel *my* support?

Chapter Seven

Envy, Jealousy, and Competition

A true friend stabs you in the front.
—OSCAR WILDE

RIGHT HERE, *in the middle of paradise, Wendy felt devastated.*
She came to this fabulous ocean resort in Cancún with her clos-
est friends from work expecting abundant sunshine, fabulous food,
a booming nightlife, and maybe a sexy dancing partner or two.
She'd gotten all of that and it felt luxurious—until ten minutes ago
when she learned what Shelly had been saying.

"She's arrogant and needs to be in charge of everything."

Wendy had gone for a quiet margarita by the bar. The other
women were dancing up a storm, but after four full days and
nights Wendy wanted something approaching downtime. Of course,
that meant fending off the advances of a couple of men, but Wendy
knew how to keep guys at bay when she wasn't interested. She
glanced back at her group all dancing together and noticed Shelly
talking animatedly to the others, but gave it little thought. Espe-
cially because none of the girls seemed particularly interested in
what Shelly had to say.

"I don't have any idea why men think she's soooo gorgeous."

Wendy relaxed with her drink and thought about how she'd put
the trip together. Christie actually mentioned it first, but once all the

women decided they loved the idea, Wendy took charge. It always seemed to be that way. Wendy took naturally to leadership—she was manager of their sales team at work, after all—and she had fun planning things for herself and others. After a little bit of intense Internet surfing, a couple of phone calls, and a "team meeting" her boss definitely wouldn't have approved, Wendy had everyone booked into a top hotel on the beach (at a bargain price, of course), set up excursions for parasailing, snorkeling, and exploring Aztec ruins, and arranged VIP passes to one of the hottest clubs in Mexico. The others seemed thrilled, and Wendy was more than a little satisfied with her efforts.

She looked over at the dancing circle. Most of the women were moving less fervently now, and Shelly seemed seriously worked up about something.

"You know why she's not dancing with us? Because she wants to hog all of the men to herself!"

Wendy wondered what had Shelly so upset. She'd rarely seen her like this. In fact, when they went out as a group, Shelly was usually the quietest and most reserved. She'd go out on the dance floor with the rest of them, and she seemed to have a good time, but she shrunk away at other times and never seemed to send out the right signals to men.

Wendy had never had that problem in her life. Even when she was in her early teens, she had guys after her at every turn. When she looked in the mirror, she knew she looked okay, but she never went out of her way to flaunt her looks. If anything, she tended to downplay her appearance, opting to dress down as much as she could in her surroundings. In fact, she sort of thought of herself as a tomboy, much more comfortable in an oversized T-shirt than a cocktail dress.

Still, that didn't prevent the men from calling, even when she just wanted to be alone with her friends. Wendy was convinced that kind of attention was the reason she'd cycled through so many female friends over the years, and she finally decided to do something about it. She started holding parties to bring her ample guy network together with her circle of female friends. It didn't always work, though. Just a couple of weeks ago, one of the men was particularly dismissive to the shy and delicate Shelly, leaving her embarrassed and humiliated.

Wendy wondered if Shelly was recounting that experience to the others on the dance floor and if that was the reason for her fervor. Once again, Wendy turned to look for her friends—only to discover that Christie was walking toward her while Shelly was trudging off toward her room.

"You won't believe what's been going on since you left," Christie said, rolling her eyes.

Wendy felt a little apprehensive. "What?"

"Shelly just went off on you. I mean completely and totally off."

Wendy pivoted toward where she'd last seen Shelly, but she was already gone. "She did what?"

"You'd barely made it to the bar when Shelly started spouting. It was like she was possessed or something."

For the next several minutes, Christie told Wendy everything that her friend said about her. The words were ugly and Wendy felt physically assaulted. She'd always been on Shelly's side. She always tried to help her.

"Finally," Christie said, "we told her we were here for a good time not another one of her miserable gossip sessions. That's when she stomped off." Christie gazed over at the exit. "I think she hates us now as much as she hates you."

Wendy's heart felt leaden. "How could she?" she said shakily. But deep down, Wendy knew exactly how.

Jealousy and Competition

So very many women, even my own sister, tell me that envy and jealousy in women (as opposed to men), tend to be about not belonging to the "in crowd," to a lack of harmony in the circle of friends, or all of that adding up to a lack of security in a woman's sense of being "normal" as judged by a group. My sister says, "If one woman gets way more attention from men than another, it's not pretty. Sometimes it's about a job, but usually it's men. Your friends are a reflection on *you*. If your girlfriends are friends with assholes, chances are there are similarities and you don't want to be friends with those girls. *Women need to feel they are 'normal.'*"

The solution, she says, is to surround herself with friends who are real and humble, not arrogant. She says this makes it likely that everyone will "find a guy who is their type rather than hogging all the attention. It's about options. Also, when someone is on a power kick, or tries dominating everything, it's not good. We need the yin and yang, and balance—an attention hog throws things off balance."

If friendship is a woman's source of power in life and the road to a happy, successful destiny is through the way you employ your own character in them, then envy and jealousy are perhaps the scariest secret emotional enemies of your growth.

For women, competition may be about where you are with yourself. Many women are only competitive when they feel good about themselves. This, however, takes us into the domains of the mammalian and higher brains. The girl on top, unlike the top "alpha male," may not feel good about having that rank because in many cases it takes away some of the safeness of belonging she once enjoyed.

Competition for women in the workplace is far more about higher-brain personality type. A Warrior woman in a law firm may be vigorously competitive, whereas one with a Lover temperament may not compete with anyone but herself. Down at the primal, female reptilian-brain level, though, it's about belonging, normalcy, and harmony versus exclusion, ostracism, and disorder.

It's about multiple, joined circles of friends. Women are more se-cure when they belong to triangles within circles of friends, linked to circles within triangles of other circles. However, jealousy and envy undermine this.

The Three Brains of Jealousy

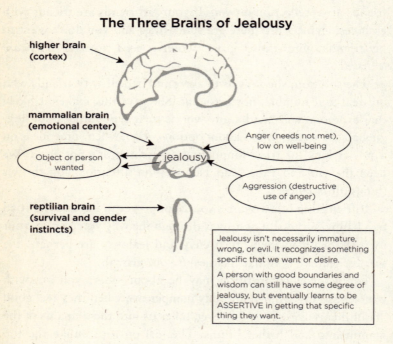

higher brain
(cortex)

mammalian brain
(emotional center)

Object or person
wanted

jealousy

Anger (needs not met),
low on well-being

Aggression (destructive
use of anger)

reptilian brain
(survival and gender
instincts)

Jealousy isn't necessarily immature, wrong, or evil. It recognizes something specific that we want or desire.

A person with good boundaries and wisdom can still have some degree of jealousy, but eventually learns to be ASSERTIVE in getting that specific thing they want.

Jealousy is an angry, negative emotion directed at a wish for or want of something specific we do not have. A jealous person may be mature or immature, wise or foolish, and may act on her jeal-ousy or not. Regardless, jealousy informs us of what we do not have but want. As we will soon see, there is a cure for jealousy in using the energy in your anger to go after exactly what you want.

Envy is a related, but more global, challenge to friendship—an angry emotional state not necessarily directed at acquiring anything

The Three Brains of Envy

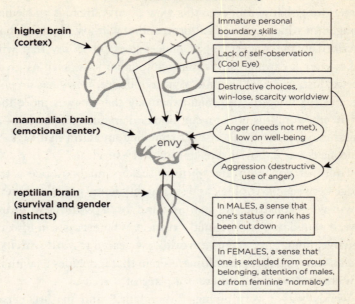

higher brain
(cortex)

Immature personal
boundary skills

Lack of self-observation
(Cool Eye)

Destructive choices,
win-lose, scarcity worldview

mammalian brain
(emotional center)

Anger (needs not met),
low on well-being

envy

Aggression (destructive
use of anger)

reptilian brain
(survival and gender
instincts)

In MALES, a sense that
one's status or rank has
been cut down

In FEMALES, a sense that
one is excluded from group
belonging, attention of males,
or from feminine "normalcy"

specific but fueled by both the reptilian brain's spark of passion and a lack of sophisticated higher-brain boundaries, ethics, or constructive wisdom.

For both men and women, envy can come in two forms: mere emotional hatred based on a sense of lacking and passionate hatred based on both emotional lack and the loss of gender-based status or belonging. The former is mammalian-brained only. The latter is charged with both the mammalian brain's emotion of hate and the reptilian brain's instincts toward masculinity, femininity, and survival.

Envy is one of the "seven deadly sins" but is unique among them. Chaucer described envy as sadness at goodness or prosperity in another person and happiness at their failure or downfall. It is interesting that within even this view of envy, there is an element of anger (of which sadness is a form) and of win-lose thinking, both described in the Anger Map. Chaucer goes on to say that what makes envy a cardinal sin is that while other sins (such as greed, avarice, lust, or pride) have an "object of desire," envy has no positive aim for the self. You might then say that envy is more than just an emotion. It is both an emotion and an outright passion—an immature, dysfunctional, instinct sounding an alarm that says, "If someone else is happy, it threatens my very survival."

Those of you who are spiritual seekers might notice a true bridge between psychology and spirituality in my model: whatever is win-win, constructive, mature, and of a worldview geared toward abundance is a spiritual "virtue." Whatever is win-lose, destructive, immature, and of a worldview geared toward scarcity is a "sin." Envy is, then, the ultimate sin in that it deludes us with the view that the world out there is a place of scarcity.

Wendy was a very giving, "abundant," and mature person for the most part, whose tragic flaw was needing to belong too much, to the point of trying so hard to win friends (for instance, bringing her women friends together to meet her men friends) that it sabotaged her. In some sense, her feminine reptilian-brain need to belong got the best of her better judgment. Shelly, on the other hand, was the envious one, who tore apart the reputation of a friend needlessly, out of a sense of scarcity regarding the number of available men for her in the world. She defeated her own potential to learn the skills of attraction from a friend (Wendy) who was an unwitting master of them. In doing so, she also likely ruined her own reputation among her circle of friends. Who would trust her to keep secrets about *them* after her gossiping rampage?

To continue the psychology/spirituality model, if our reptilian brains are left to their own devices, we are akin to animals and "living in sin." We need the higher brain's ability with boundaries to be truly mature, psychologically *and* spiritually, to keep the survival instinct in the reptilian brain from driving us to unregulated self-preservation that stomps over the rights and feelings of others. Having our Cool Eye turned on serves us well in our quest for a better life through the power of friendship and a destiny determined by a higher character. With this core higher-brain skill, we can "see" what is going on under the hood of our minds so we don't fall prey to impulses to steal, destroy, lie, or feel envy.

As you can see in the diagram, since envy is technically an emotion, it is located in the mammalian brain. Yet, it is the master of negative emotions, deserving of the lowest level of Chaucer's hell, influenced strongly by effects of the other two brains as well. It

The Three Brains of Envy

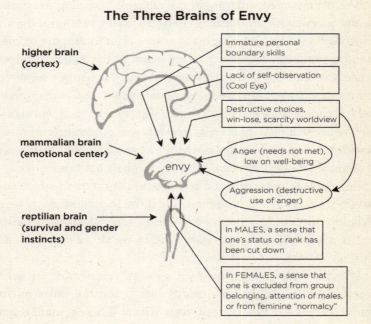

higher brain (cortex)

Immature personal boundary skills

Lack of self-observation (Cool Eye)

Destructive choices, win-lose, scarcity worldview

mammalian brain (emotional center)

Anger (needs not met), low on well-being

envy

Aggression (destructive use of anger)

reptilian brain (survival and gender instincts)

In MALES, a sense that one's status or rank has been cut down

In FEMALES, a sense that one is excluded from group belonging, attention of males, or from feminine "normalcy" plays out in slightly different ways for women and men but universally carries with it a lack of self-knowledge (poor Cool Eye ability); a personal boundary riddled with holes, which causes the envious person to disrespect the rights, opinions, ownership, and personal experience of others; and a childlike worldview of helpless scarcity that drives destructive, win-lose social interactions. In this area, Chaucer was a bit off target in finding that the envious have no desired object of envy. They do and it is invisible: the self-esteem energy called well-being, taken at the expense of others—through guilt trips, gossip, slander, and even crimes of hate.

The Terrible Destructive Power of Envy in Depression

The definition of suffering in my model is "wishing to control the uncontrollable" or "burning energy on trying to control the uncontrollable" in life. If we were to go now right to the core of envy in the mammalian brain by looking again at the Anger Map, we would see that envy is just a form of suffering. It is anger we direct at a future (that we do not control) in which we suspect that others will have more than us; therefore, if we carry with us a worldview that we live in a place of scarcity, our future is predetermined to see us with less, our needs unmet no matter what we do. We are doomed to even less of our needs being fulfilled if others have more.

Envy is aggression directed at a view of the future in which you imagine others having more than you: more happiness, more love, and more success. It is also by definition a form of suffering (wishing to control the uncontrollable) since we do not control the future. *Assertiveness* is the cure.

When we are angry, depressed, violent, or envious, we carry negative energy. When that energy bleeds out the holes in our boundary toward others, it stresses them. When it manages to

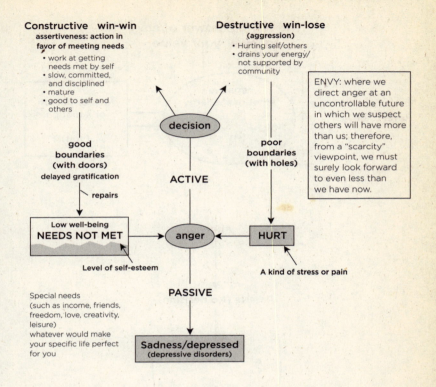

Constructive win-win
assertiveness: action in
favor of meeting needs
- work at getting
  needs met by self
- slow, committed,
  and disciplined
- mature
- good to self and
  others

Destructive win-lose
(aggression)
- Hurting self/others
- drains your energy/
  not supported by
  community

ENVY: where we
direct anger at an
uncontrollable future
in which we suspect
others will have more
than us; therefore,
from a "scarcity"
viewpoint, we must
surely look forward
to even less than
we have now.

**good
boundaries
(with doors)**
delayed gratification

**poor
boundaries
(with holes)**

repairs

ACTIVE

decision

Low well-being
NEEDS NOT MET

anger

HURT

Level of self-esteem

A kind of stress or pain

Special needs
(such as income, friends,
freedom, love, creativity,
leisure)
whatever would make
your specific life perfect
for you

PASSIVE

Sadness/depressed
(depressive disorders)

stress them for long enough and busts traumatically into their
boundaries or creeps through the holes in their own boundaries
(the buttons we "push" in others) we have aggressed them and our
value in what once was a friendship has dropped in their eyes (or
rather, their mammalian brain).

Depression is anger and anger is depression. Many psychologists observe that it is more common for women to express depression in words and outward feelings and for men to express it in
aggressive acts. With your understanding of the reptilian-brain
differences between us, you know why.

The terrible power of envy
to lower your value

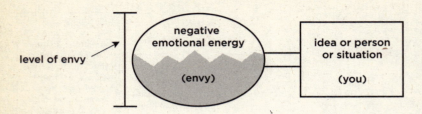

level of envy

negative
emotional energy

(envy)

idea or person
or situation

(you)

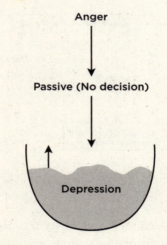

Anger

↓

Passive (No decision)

↓

Depression

A Depression Tank: Stored-up Anger

All depression is simply anger.

So very many times in psychiatric practice, one sees this sce-
nario: two women, both of equal intelligence and experience, work
in similar jobs for the same company. One is offered a promotion

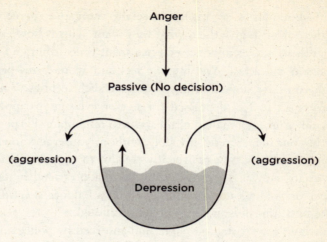

A Depression Tank: Stored-up Anger
All depression is simply anger.

and the other is not. Whether envy ensues is not at all a matter of whether the boss is being "fair"—except that said boss is likely more engaged in friendship with the promoted woman than with the woman not promoted. The prime driver of whether envy arises is in the character of the envious. Some of us might feel quite angry, and righteously indignant, that we were not promoted when we are just as smart, just as talented, and just as senior as the person who was. "It isn't fair!" we protest. Life, while not "fair," most certainly and with scientific precision runs on the clockwork of friendship.

Here is the psychology of what is *really* going on in "life's unfairness." People who are envious today were likely envious the day before and the day before that. They carry anger around with them, and it bleeds out through holes in their boundaries that they don't even see. Their Cool Eye is chronically turned off. They trip over the boundaries of others and unwittingly dump their anger into the boundaries of others, especially those they perceive to have the power to give them what they want. This is how envy is an aggressive act, as anyone who has spent time around an envious person can attest. You literally feel bad around this person, though you have done nothing to deserve such feelings. You can actually start to feel depressed *for* her or even guilt-tripped *by* her. Soon, your mammalian brain starts to retabulate this person's value in your life, secretly, invisibly, without you even knowing it is happening. She is now of even lower value to you, a lesser friend today than she was yesterday. Soon, there is no friendship at all. The person is like a number in the red on a balance sheet. If you are the boss, this person does not get promoted.

Fair laws are written on paper and enforced by police and the courts. There are no such laws in friendship, emotional politics, or the social jungles of dating, the workplace, and recreational venues. As Francis Edward Smedley wrote, "All's fair in love and war." Now you know why. Love and hate, friendship and value are located only in the domain of the mammalian brain. Rights, laws, and résumés are the stuff of the higher brain's intellect and boundary function. We need all three brains, of course, to be civilized and complete human beings, but this "lawless" aspect of human emotional politics is the reason there is so much confusion in our friendships and especially in youth who struggle to figure out how they fit into the social circles of school and the workplace.

The Only Cure for Envy, Jealousy, and Destructive Competition

In the example of the job promotion above, the woman with the most mature worldview—one of abundance—and with the best boundaries, moral judgment, constructiveness, a win-win attitude, and, ultimately, the most positive emotion to offer the boss, was, among two otherwise equally qualified candidates, the one who got the promotion. The boss will never admit, maybe not even to herself, that she promoted a person for reasons other than protocol, résumé, or company policy, but we all instinctively know why she did.

If the woman not promoted could turn on her Cool Eye and look detachedly at the situation, she would have a wonderful chance to learn and grow from it—to take an angry, depressing, envious experience and turn it to a positive one. She might move from the scarcity of the upper right arm of the Anger Map, create a better boundary, and shift over to the upper left arm, where the ultimate cure for anger, nonbiological depression, and the aggression of envy lies in the win-win, abundant, constructive option we all have for dealing with anger, called *assertiveness*.

Assertiveness is *going after what you want* by using your anger in a mature way that *empowers your self-reliance and self-sufficiency*, and gets your own needs met *without disrespecting, using, or abusing* others. The secret psychology of assertiveness is that every time you use it (as opposed to depressive reveries or aggressive, envious guilt trips) you will in fact, 100 percent of the time, fill your own boundary up with an equal amount of well-being, one of the two components of self-esteem. Your needs will be met—as many of them as you like, as long as they are reasonable and not dependent on the actions of specific other people. Self-esteem is the energy that grows new friendships in your life. It is what is exchanged when we love friends and romantic partners. So with assertiveness not only will your needs be met (by you), but you will ironically find yourself surrounded by even more friends. All by doing this for yourself.

Shelly, for example, could have found this in her romantic life. Had she been constructive and abundant rather than envious of Wendy, she might have studied what it is about Wendy that is so alluring to men. Maybe she would have found that she is just as attractive to men as Wendy when she has a smile of abundant expectation on her face. And she would have kept Wendy as a friend. She would be better off today, and in the future, than she was with the brief boost of self-esteem that comes from one-upping others through envious, aggressive acts like slanderous gossip.

The friendship triangles and circles for the unpromoted woman above likewise have two possible outcomes.

In the first diagram, notice how the unpromoted but envious woman with poor boundaries and destructive use of anger (envy and aggression) devalues herself enough to become an outcast from the local politics of what was once a friendship triad. The other two women instinctively move away from her psychologically. Her friend is promoted to higher status in the company and in friendship is more on par (a favorite) with the boss. Her value is higher in friendship to the boss. But continued further, the unpromoted friend will not only have excluded herself from the politics and circle of friendship but may even be fired. None of this, of course, is explained in any employee handbook or corporate protocol, but it is the real and invisible psychology of envy in office politics. Now it is visible for you.

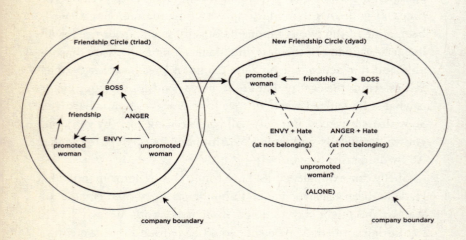

Envy and anger become even more passionately amplified—and hateful—when the feminine reptilian-brain need for connection and belonging is severed. The new friendship circle where the woman is promoted to engage in greater teamwork with the boss insulates them both from the stress thrown at them from the unpromoted woman. But, again, if the woman who was not promoted keeps it up, she may not only be left out of the exclusive group of her superiors, she may be fired.

What if, instead, the unpromoted woman's higher brain was skilled and mature?

If the woman who wasn't promoted does not succumb to envy, learns lessons from her friend, and maintains a friendship with both her friend and her boss, she is more likely to get promoted at some

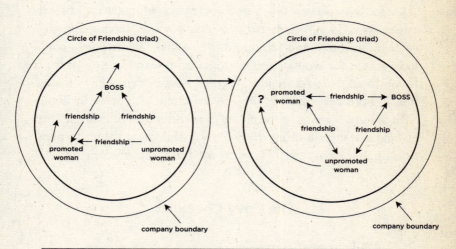

Note how, if the unpromoted woman does not succumb to ENVY, learns lessons from her friend, and maintains friendship with both her friend and boss, she is even MORE likely to get promoted at some point in the future and still enjoy belonging to both the circle of politics and to the company.

Also note that the unpromoted woman will still have to maintain positive energy through assertiveness, even though she desired and did not get promoted, YET. This maintains friendship and even encourages both friend and boss to "cheer for her" in doing her own work to get to her personal reward.

point in the future. She still enjoys belonging to both the circle of politics and to the company. The unpromoted woman will still have to maintain positive energy through assertiveness, even though she desired and did not get a promotion. This maintains friendship and even encourages both her friend and her boss to cheer for her.

When you have a mature, constructive, win-win worldview geared toward abundance, instead of envy you see that there is more than enough to go around for us all. The unpromoted woman who values her friend and values herself enough not to suffer over the future through envy, can see that if her friend with identical skill and talent gets promoted, that must mean that she can, too. Some way, somehow, and at some time, she can and will advance in her career. The promotion of her friend is a hopeful message to her rather than a source of competitive sadness.

Assertiveness is the only direct route to building the type of self-esteem we call well-being, that emotional sense of "having enough," of being nurtured and feeling "full" (of life). Assertiveness could have gotten the woman above a raise or at least have given her a lesson to apply to future jobs. It could have gotten Shelly satisfaction in both her romantic life and her circle of friends, including with Wendy. It is one of the pillars of friendships, political stability, lasting romances and marriages, successful careers and corporations, public works, and character itself. Character is destiny.

The Envy Checklist

- Am I envious?

- Where am I in need? Do I lack assertiveness in those areas?

- If so, I will look at the positive aspects I lack but the person I have envy toward uses to her advantage, assertively build them into my life, and look forward to a bright future.

Chapter Eight

Friendship Dilemmas

*Advice is like snow; the softer it falls, the longer it
dwells upon, and the deeper it sinks into the mind.*
— SAMUEL TAYLOR COLERIDGE

ONE OF the great obstacles women face in friendship is that of
making a social choice, one that can at times rattle or even end
some relationships. As you are finding with nearly any situation
involving the analysis and repair of friendship problems, all three
brains matter. Women, because of their special innate biological
sensitivity to important relationships, may at times find themselves
in passionate turmoil over friendship dilemmas: decisions that could
involve the end of (or at least greatly damage) a relationship or
cause pain, sadness, or anxiety to others. Luckily, we already have
all the tools we need to light up the invisible complexity of these
dilemmas and make them simple and therefore solvable.

Friends vs. Family

Kim was a stylist at a salon in a small town in New Jersey. She
worked long hours establishing her client base, and when she got
a chance to socialize, it was like Christmas for her. During her late
twenties, she gathered a tight group of friends around her. The big

event for Kim was the monthly trip she made with those friends to New York City, for a night on the town.

This month was going to be different, though. It was early autumn, winter would come soon, and the women had all decided that it was time for a "girls' vacation" to Lake Powell, Arizona. There would be warm sun, boys, and three days of social paradise. Kim's eyes lit up when she got the invitation, but as she scanned the dates they planned to be gone, there was a dreadful problem. Well, not so dreadful. Joyous actually. It was the weekend of her mother's fiftieth birthday.

Kim thought about how it might affect her mom and her married brothers for her to be gone during such a special time. Then she thought about the next five snowy months, when it will be difficult to venture out and there will be so many fewer guys out and available. Her friends would beg and plead with her to go to Lake Powell, and some of them might even hate her for not going to such a rare event.

Kim was good at turning on her Cool Eye for important decisions, and she realized that she had to navigate between long-term and short-term views of her relationships. Lake Powell would be very enticing, but there would be many more trips for her. She had been through many friendships that worked, some that had failed, and she knew that there were always more friends to be had. She would only have one mom turning fifty. There was nothing else to think about. She would stay to celebrate.

As we learned in the myth of Demeter and Persephone, women are tied for life in one form or another to their mothers. Yet Kim's case shows a woman with a choice between her own needs, the approval of her friends, and not just her mom, but her entire family. The Demeter and Persephone myth shows women an organic, harmonious option for navigating between husband and mother (she splits her time between both). It also helps us address our connections between friends and family. Women are gifted at finding

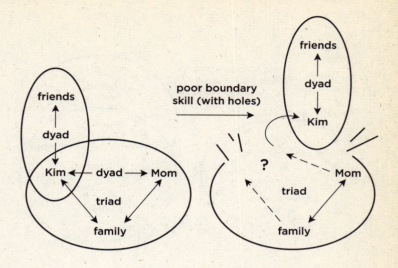

connection and harmony, joining circles to circles, and working within relationship triangles if their higher-brain boundary maturity is up to the task. But not if they have weak boundaries with holes in them.

One solution to Kim's dilemma between mom and friends would be to suggest to her family that they throw the party in Lake Powell. Mom would be reminded that fifty is not really that old these days, Kim's brothers and their families would enjoy a break in some warm weather, and Kim could invite her friends to her mom's birthday festivities as well.

In joining circles to other circles that preserve the triangle's stability and harmony, Kim, like all of us, would find the means of harnessing the power of friendship, a system that maintains the good boundaries of relationship triangles and accesses the synergy of multiple groups' energy, the circles of friends. This is the invisible psychology of all mature leaders.

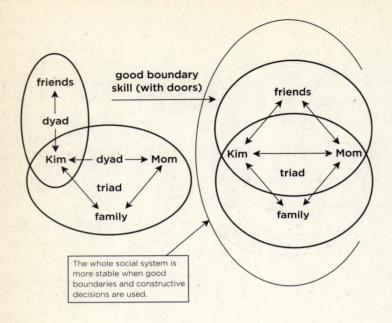

The whole social system is more stable when good boundaries and constructive decisions are used.

Imagine circles upon circles of self-esteem energy, joined by the architecture of good boundaries in the triangles they form—all with you at the center. When you are all alone in a life without friends, and therefore without love, you are psychologically very much like a one-celled organism. You are technically alive but very fragile, easily burst apart by toxins and trauma, and frustrated with your ability to grow if there isn't immediate nourishment in the vicinity. But if you look at a circle of friends as a single living being itself—whether it contains men or women or both—it becomes like a multicelled organism, a fully functioning living thing immune to the stresses of a foul-weather environment and attacks from hostile forces, and inside itself a wellspring of creativity, innovation, safety, belonging, and potency.

Friends vs. Your Man

Before learning the power of friendship networks, at some point almost every woman falls hard for a man, to the neglect of her friends. Siobhan was that girl. She was born in Moira, Northern Ireland, and when she was thirteen her father got a promotion with his software company that led the whole family to a small town in northern California. A number of years would pass before she could feel comfortable in her new surroundings, but by then she was ready to go to college.

When she entered her freshman year at the University of California, San Francisco, she made the kind of friend she always thought she would have for life. Debbie was in several of her journalism classes and was everything Siobhan was not—an outgoing, wild and crazy party girl who always had positive things to say when Siobhan felt especially down or challenged. They were together nearly every day.

When Kevin came into Siobhan's life for the first time at the spring social, she was stunned. Siobhan had not dated at all in high school and only lightly through most of the first year of college. Shy as she was, Kevin saw through her seeming aloofness to find a good heart, and he was very slow and patient at getting to know her. Right from the start, she felt safe with him.

Siobhan methodically cut off from Debbie to be with Kevin nearly all the time. Although Siobhan did this with no malice toward Debbie—she never made a conscious decision to spend less time with Debbie at all—Debbie was quite hurt. Even their telephone contact tapered off over the next two months. As a result, Debbie slowly realized that she would have to continue not only building new friendships as satisfying as the one she had with Siobhan but also finding a new best friend.

Six months later, Siobhan awoke in her dorm room to find Kevin hadn't come home. She sensed that something was very wrong. It wasn't like him not to call. When she confronted Kevin, he was very vague and evaded the details of where he had been, claiming he had to go to class and would speak with her about it later that evening. Siobhan suddenly found herself thinking of Debbie all day and wishing they had the easy contact they shared when school started.

When she met with Kevin later that evening for dinner in the cafeteria, he explained that he had simply been out late with the guys and didn't want to barge in and wake her at that hour. She felt the restraint in his voice and resolved not to press the matter further for now. Yet Siobhan yearned to talk to someone, anyone, about her lingering worry.

The next week, Kevin didn't call Siobhan for three nights in a row and of course didn't sleep over, a marked departure from their habit. During the last of these nights, Siobhan texted him five times. Finally, about three hours later, near midnight, he called to ask what the matter was. He said he was "studying very hard" for finals. Then he made a strange sound, a kind of half laugh, distracted and cut short, as if clearing his throat before hanging up.

Siobhan sat there into the wee hours of the morning, staring into the bulb of her fluorescent light, wondering what the sound was and whether there was another woman with Kevin right now.

She really needed Debbie.

Siobhan picked up the phone to call her and found Debbie drowsy on the other end. After a brief, courteous conversation, Debbie told her that she too had a boyfriend but was getting her academic act together and needed to go. She did not go into detail or talk to her former best friend about romantic challenges, leaving Siobhan feeling frustrated and quite alone, the same feeling of not belonging that she had had upon arriving in the United States so long ago.

The next week, Siobhan saw Kevin walking across campus with another girl. He had not called in five days nor even bothered to tell her that he wanted to break up.

But romance is not what we are examining here. I raise the failure of Siobhan and Kevin's relationship to show a second, more disastrous and devastating habit that appears in the lives of many women in their late-adolescent, early adult years. In going overboard in their devotion for a man, many women neglect their sisterhood with other women. The personal boundary provides a way for women to navigate between the absolute need to champion and admire a man for the sake of romance and the need to remain solid in a network of circles of friendship.

The prime difficulty for Siobhan in her triangle with Debbie and Kevin was not as much her boundary as it was her general

Dyadic relationships have bad boundaries with "holes"

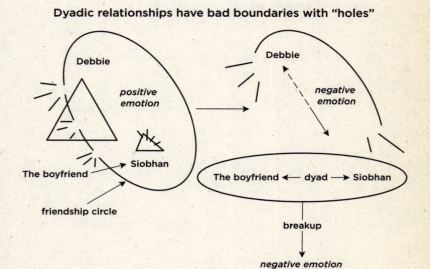

passiveness and a failure to use her Cool Eye. We learned in the early chapters that all of our decisions are either constructive or destructive, or aren't really decisions but passivity. We also observed that being passive leaves us a little "less alive" (remember that biologists define life as "irritable" or "that which makes decisions about the environment").

When we do nothing about the situations and dilemmas that come at us in friendship, our life secretly, silently, invisibly goes downhill. Our social groups change around us. People join and leave. We grow into new duties, responsibilities, and tastes in life, and some of our friends change in their feelings about us. That

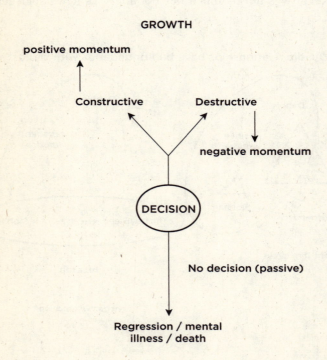

doesn't mean we have to stop being friends with these people alto-gether, but rather that they drop down a little on the friendship spectrum, away from "best friend."

In the diagram you see the effect of *momentum* or *habit* in friend-ship. Momentum and habit are simply a tendency to consistently employ a *type of decision strategy* in particular circumstances. For example, you may have some friends who are consistently late or hold grudges over small infractions. These are *destructive habits* and create *negative momentum* for their friendships. If they persist, the friendships will die because there is a regular introduction of negative emotional energy into them. On the other hand, you may have friends who are habitual smilers. They consistently ask how you are doing before they talk about themselves, and they do this with everyone they meet. These are *constructive habits* and create *positive momentum* for their friendships. Even if these people get off on the wrong foot with new friends, their good upward friend-ship momentum will likely get the new friends to come around to a solid connection and growth together.

Now the great thing about being willing to make tough deci-sions about the dilemmas in our lives is that even our mistakes give us information. They tell us what doesn't work, what offends people, what pleases people, what benefits us after the fact, and what seemed harmless but hurts us after the fact. If your Cool Eye is on as much as possible, you can and will learn from the mis-taken decisions and even learn to reverse them, fix them, or pre-vent them the moment they occur. This is how we grow as people in mature friendships. Most people feel good about forgiving oth-ers. This provides a boost of good energy and self-esteem that adds even more positive emotion to the connections we share.

Learning from mistakes actually gives us two new inner resources for friendship: *conscience* and *intuition*.

Any decision about a dilemma is better than no decision at all. Living in passivity is like being barely alive. Why? Because every

The Types of Decisions and Detail of the Decision Spectrum

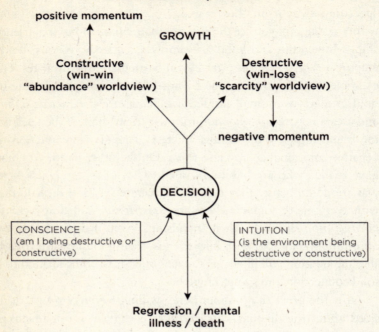

positive momentum

GROWTH

Constructive
(win-win
"abundance" worldview)

Destructive
(win-lose
"scarcity" worldview)

negative momentum

DECISION

CONSCIENCE
(am I being destructive or
constructive)

INTUITION
(is the environment being
destructive or constructive)

Regression / mental
illness / death

decision we make—good or bad, constructive or destructive, out of poor ethics or naïveté—gives us new information.

Think of us as being born with two empty tanks labeled "conscience" and "intuition." We don't know right from wrong yet, and we certainly aren't able to deduce sophisticated solutions to complex friendship situations. How in the world are we supposed to fill up those tanks?

The answer is to make lots and lots of decisions in various environments and situations, and to learn from your mistakes. When you do wrong to someone and it hurts her, you learn in your conscience (if your Cool Eye is on) not to do it again. Likewise, if you do something that pleases someone and makes her smile, you realize that you ought to do it many times again because you did "right" ethically.

If you make a decision to move to Montana when deep down you love the urban life, it won't be long until you realize that you lacked good intuition in making that move. You move back to New York and realize that it suited you all along. Likewise, if you have an inner sense that you love animals and have a chance to move to Montana, your Cool Eye, if it is turned on, can call your attention to the opportunity. You find that you are in paradise because there are many jobs working with horse ranches. You look back and say, "I had a hunch this would be good for me."

When our tanks of conscience and intuition are relatively full and equal in balance, then we are *wise*, and our wisdom is a reliable force in making decisions in our lives, even in the midst of terrible dilemmas. We have "been here before" and we know the right answer to the dilemma, even if we don't like having to go through some temporary discomfort to get to a peaceful solution.

Siobhan put herself in a difficult situation with Debbie. She passively went along with what life presented her, not truly committing to choose Kevin over Debbie or Debbie over Kevin. This is a silent, invisible, insidious process for most of us. We don't realize that we are letting our lives stagnate (the world gives us only its leftovers when we are passive) or that we are depriving ourselves of a chance to develop our conscience and intuition. We are denying the only chances in life we have for growing wise, which will make every subsequent decision we make so much more on target, right, and beneficial to both our friends and ourselves.

While Siobhan was not very good at using boundaries to find a balance between choosing a man versus a friend (and keeping ties to both), ultimately there will be times when a man absolutely does not get along with a best friend, and you really will have to choose one over the other. This is where even with great boundaries and the ability to find harmony between people you will need the conscience, intuition, and wisdom to know which person to keep in your life. Your experience will guide you.

You still need sisterhood even after you are committed to a man. To cut those ties to your circles of friends not only shows your man that your boundaries are poor, but it separates you from the core reptilian-brain feminine need for belonging, in the spirit of Hestia. Remember the other myths that explain the feminine reptilian brain as well. Psyche could not have learned the true nature of her husband without the (admittedly meddling) intervention of her sisters, and even when she was married to Hades, Persephone emerged to the surface of the world for two thirds of every year.

Friends vs. Your Job

Writer Rannveig Traustadóttir says:

Women typically describe their friendships in terms of closeness and emotional attachment. What characterizes friendships between women is the willingness to share important feelings, thoughts, experiences, and support. Women devote a good deal of time and intensity of involvement to friends. Friendships between women, more so than between men, are broad and less likely to be segmented.

It makes sense, then, that while men often concentrate their friendships in activities that inevitably relate to career aspirations, women value and attend to friendship in ways that might sometimes place them in a dilemma between being a good friend and a good career woman.

Joanna was a bright and attractive woman in her late thirties. She had been married for two years, and she had given birth to a beautiful son a year before she returned to her career as an accountant with a large Wall Street firm. Within six months, she was humming along again, rejuvenated as a mom and a professional.

Joanna's friend Karen had been there for her through thick and thin over the past decade since they met while working for the same brokerage. Both were single at the time, and they bonded deeply while navigating the single life in Philadelphia. Karen was also married now, but she had decided to work just a couple more years on her career before establishing a larger family. Hard-driving but friendly, she was a perfect complement to Joanna's softer, peaceful nature.

When Karen found a job in her firm that was perfect for Joanna, a step up in title and quite a bit more income, she called Joanna immediately to tell her to pull out her résumé. She thought it would be great for the two of them to work at the same firm again, especially since, given Joanna's family responsibilities, they had not shared as much time recently as they had in the past. Joanna accepted the gift from her friend—the type of gift that can only come in tight friendship circles.

As life moves forward, offering new lessons, we sometimes change at different speeds than even our closest friends. Not long after arriving at the new firm, Joanna noticed things about Karen that she hadn't before. For one, Joanna's new position was just one little rung above Karen's, and they had never been in that situation before. They were always buddies in their circles or partners in the same role when they did work together. Joanna wasn't Karen's immediate supervisor now, but she did have some peripheral authority over the outcome of her reports.

Karen was a very direct boss with her underlings. The directness that seemed to Joanna bold and attractive in their friendship when they were both single now sometimes felt a bit mean and uncalled for. When one day the numbers just didn't add up, Joanna had to zero in on the source—and it appeared to be Karen's team.

When she found a quiet moment to ask Karen how the numbers on the recent report could look so out of place, Karen took offense. "I got you this job," she said. "How could you even ask such a question?" Joanna had felt it was harmless enough to ask, especially with the environment in accounting being so rigorous about methods in recent years. Karen ended their brief conversation by telling Joanna that she had used formulas that were common in their particular company.

Soon after, though, one of the partners called Joanna into his office to talk about Karen's performance. "Do you think that something, to put it bluntly, is not on the up and up about Karen's methods?" he asked. This was one of those dilemmas in friendship that was not just about choosing a friend over something else. It was about being true to one's self and doing right instead of wrong. Joanna asked the partner if she could have some time to go over the report with Karen. After all, she was not an immediate supervisor, and she was relatively new to the company. "Well, that's why I'm coming to you. I understand that you are friends outside of the firm, and we have ways of doing things here, ethically, that can make waves through the rest of the department. We don't want that exactly."

As he did this, he had a strange look in his eyes. Something felt cold about him, different from the way he was during their interviews and during the introductory lunch she shared with him. She could not place what it was. He dressed the same, looked the same, had the same tone of voice and little habits like tapping his pen annoyingly as he talked. She could only feel something in her gut. An intuition.

That night, Joanna called Karen to get real about what was going on. Was Karen doing something wrong? Joanna didn't know, and it wasn't her place—in her view—to be the ultimate judge of someone else's ethics, especially without full understanding of the "methods" in question. Karen blurted out that she had heard her friend had gone into the partner's office that day. "Why are you starting a witch hunt?" she said. "I got you this job and you take it and betray me, sneaking around behind my back like that just to make yourself look good!"

Click.

Joanna rose the next day, after a restless night's sleep, with an idea. She would be *both* a good friend *and* a career woman of principles. She practiced what she would say repeatedly until she realized that this was just not her problem. *Her* job was her responsibility, not her *friend's* job. She didn't know if Karen had done something wrong, cooked the books, or was a corporate hero or villain. What she did know was that her friend was acting differently than she ever had before.

It was hurtful, but Joanna was mature enough not to let a week of terrible communication ruin a whole friendship. Karen was certainly being an awful friend right now, but Joanna felt it was not in her to seek some sort of blind retribution over it. Maybe Karen was jealous of her slightly higher position. Maybe she felt that Joanna owed her some special favor, even an unethical one.

Joanna marched into the partner's office and told him that Karen was not interested in talking to her about the issue, that the numbers on the recent report did look off somehow, and that her recommendation was simply that they be recalculated. She was new at the company and that was the extent of her insight into the issue. Systems problems happen, and it is hard to say where along the line errors arise. A step-by-step reprocessing of the report was all that was necessary. She excused herself after simply telling the truth, leaving emotional judgments and drama out of the picture.

Over the next few months, Karen didn't talk to Joanna at all and was eventually fired. Soon, though, as Joanna continued to rise in the ranks, it was publicly revealed that the partner had been secretly mandating that the books be cooked and pressuring Karen to do so. He had been setting her up as a scapegoat all along, and she was making the numbers glaringly erroneous in the hope that others would discover it without pinning it to her.

While it was a long dry spell in their relationship, Joanna and Karen did eventually get to discuss what happened, and Karen learned that her friend had not betrayed her after all. The stress of being caught in a terrible ethical dilemma had worn away at Karen's boundary, causing her to dump her frustrations on her friend, to become paranoid, jump to conclusions, and ultimately to *project* her self-doubt and near betrayal of her own ethical standards *onto* Joanna. This entire sad event was a chance for Karen to cultivate a stronger boundary and better ethics and to learn to make better decisions.

We don't often think of conscience (ethics) as a power in our lives that can be expanded, practiced, or cultivated, but it can. As we learned in the prior dilemma, we have empty tanks when we are very young. There is no sense yet of moral right or wrong, even though we arrive in this world with survival and gender instinct. This parallels evolution itself: we grow to be adolescents who learn to master the reptilian-brain instincts of relating to the opposite sex, then young adults who learn to manage the mammalian complexities of emotions and friendships, and finally mature human adults who are self-aware, understand complex social politics, and have a fully functioning personal boundary and well-developed ethics, intuition, and intelligence.

Sometimes we have to make ethical decisions that do not bring us immediate good feelings. Sometimes (often when we are younger) we make intuitive decisions that turn out to bring terrible emotions into our lives or cut down our instinctive senses of inner femininity or masculinity. In those cases, we may say that our intuition was wrong or faulty and decide to ignore intuition in the future and revert to running our lives only by rules and regulations rather than our gut. At least rules seem to be something we can count on.

The problem with this is that all of our decisions in the dilemmas of life are dependent on an equal amount of conscience and intuition. If Joanna had been all conscience in making her decisions about Karen, she might have concluded that Karen was guilty of something dreadful. She would have reported that she was certain that Karen had done wrong; the partner would have acted on this; and Karen could have even gone to jail. There was more to Joanna, though, and there was more to her friendship with Karen. No friendship that lasts for many years is completely devoid of character. While we all may go through dark periods in life, make mistakes, regress in our level of maturity, and suffer temporary losses of consistency, mutuality, sharing, or positivity in our friendships, those of us with good character can bend a little with the outside stresses of life. With good character in our higher brains, we can "bounce back" in the process called *homeostasis*. We can be flexible and still return to balance with new life lessons and growth.

Remember, the secret psychology we are uncovering is also a quantum psychology. That means that as individuals we all fall somewhere on a spectrum between two unhealthy extremes, the center of which is health or even perfection. In the case of our higher brain's mature decision-making skills, the main skill at the center of our decision making is wisdom.

If you look at yourself and your friends at any point, you will all fall somewhere on this spectrum, from immature and imbalanced between conscience and intuition (either making a *naive* decision or a *shrewd* or even criminal decision) to making a mature, balanced decision. The latter is a decision made out of *wisdom*.

Wisdom is not the same thing as intelligence. We know many very smart people (such as those in high ranks of indicted accounting firms) who did not in the end exhibit much wisdom in their

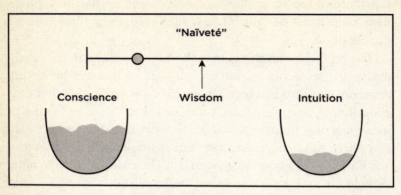

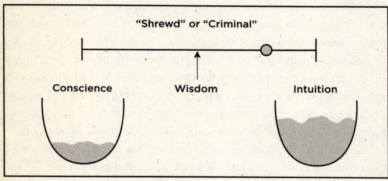

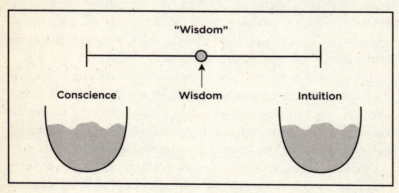

decisions. Brilliant people in the news such as Jeffrey Skilling (of Enron) come to mind or Hitler, Attila the Hun, Vlad the Impaler, or Shakespeare's Richard III. These people were in fact bright strategists but, in most cases, had very poor boundary skill that didn't respect the rights, opinions, or feeling of others. For all their brilliance, they were also fools in that they were *unwise*.

Many of us have friends who are said to be Pollyannas. They think only in moralistic black and white, failing to consider context. They may appear rigid in their morality but utterly unaware that there is a great difference between deciding to fire a gun in a crowded city street and firing one on the battlefield. There is no "right" answer to the dilemmas of life without intuition regarding the circumstances. If Joanna had worked at many different companies and seen senior intimidation, manipulation, and scapegoating happen many times, her tank of intuition would have been fuller and better equipped to spot what was going on with Karen.

Some may think that luminaries such as Mother Teresa, Gandhi, or Einstein (all universally accepted as full of wisdom) were people whose decisions were solely moral, ethical, and absolute in all circumstances.

Wisdom is that balance of conscience and intuition that we all need to know our decisions will be on the mark, leading every time to pleasant, fair, right results. Joanna had been fair, ethical, and even shrewd in placing a boundary between herself, the partner, and Karen.

Good intuition (shrewdness) says that the three lines of the relationship triangle need to be kept in mind as three separate relationships, with three separate boundary arrangements.

Without enough solid information or understanding of the situation, Joanna had no solution until she decided to let her friend and the partner's character play out their destiny together. Remembering that in relationship triangles there are always three separate relationships with group boundaries of their own, she

Relationship Triangles and Boundaries

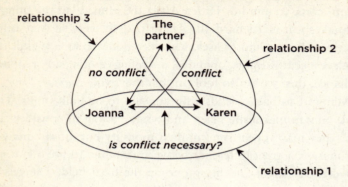

kept her decision where it belonged, inside her own boundary. This way, when the partner's character revealed his criminal activity, the connection between his relationships to Karen and Joanna dissolved, leaving the longtime friends still intact in the relationship they had enjoyed and weathered for years.

When we remember the cardinal principle of this whole book—that character is destiny, and friendship is the precise vehicle through which that destiny emerges—it becomes much easier to tolerate all the dilemmas we face. We cultivate our own character and let the dramas of even our closest friends play out the way they are meant to.

Friends vs. Your Physical Health

Tina's health had always come first in her life, before career, family, and even friendship. She ate only organic foods, exercised at least every other day, and neither drank nor smoked. This is why her friend Jennifer's dilemma was so perplexing for her.

Jennifer had lupus and a bleeding disorder. She was married with two kids but had been separated from her husband for the past year. The two women had worked side by side as emergency room technicians until layoffs happened right around the time that Jennifer's husband left her. Several times, Jennifer should have been in the hospital for flare-ups of her lupus but preferred to act as if she were not sick. Now that she was separated from her husband, she felt increasingly lonely and had a desperate need to go out again with her former single friends, drinking and smoking.

Tina had never fought with Jennifer before, but if ever there was a time to do so it was now. She understood that Jennifer didn't want anyone to think of her as "different." Yet, over the months leading up to their big blowup, Jennifer continued to ignore the signals of an impending worsening of her lupus.

One night, Jennifer called Tina to ask her about a terrible dilemma. After being out of work for a few months, she got a new job working with Tina again. She wondered if she could handle the new job and its stress, or if she should go on disability. Tina felt that Jennifer should not go on disability because it would cause her to give up freedom (and she was an awesome technician) and because she wouldn't have insurance, which she badly needed to care for herself and her children. Tina then took the opportunity to tell Jennifer that she was being horribly irresponsible in mistreating her body.

Tina had a way of being impatient with people who don't attend to their health, a character trait that had served her well on the job. There, people needed to hear the blunt truth about their health and act quickly to change their lifestyle risk factors for disease and trauma. What comes with this trait, however, is a tendency to hurt the feelings of others (at least temporarily). Hurting other people's feelings leads to negative emotion between people and, if not supported by all the other factors in the master checklist, can bring a friendship to its knees. And that's exactly what happened. Jennifer was feeling particularly vulnerable and over-sensitive, and Tina was exceptionally impatient after a long shift at work.

During their conversation, Tina confronted Jennifer with her latest lupus flare-up and took her to task for her escalating drinking and smoking. To Jennifer this felt like her friend wasn't even listening to her. She felt slapped in the face at her moment of need and conflict. Ironically, to Tina, who in her mind was only helping with a candid and honest assessment, it also felt like a slap in the face.

They didn't talk for about a week but Jennifer soon realized that a spat like this wasn't worth ruining their friendship, especially with all the challenges they both faced as young, essentially single women. Jennifer was at rock bottom, crumbling, her mind veering this way and that on virtually every decision. She swallowed her pride and called Tina to apologize.

Tina accepted the apology, and after weighing all the factors, she felt that Jennifer ought to stay on the new job to keep the insurance, completely cut out her bad habits in favor of getting care for her pain-control trouble, and start slowly making a plan for recovering some sense of social and physical stability.

Tina learned a strong lesson that her tendency toward "brutal honesty" might not have a place in *every* interaction with people—especially dear friends in trouble. She decided that she would silently lead Jennifer to the right answers: that our choices need to champion our own health and happiness first if we are to be good parents, employees, or friends.

Sometimes the most difficult dilemmas of friendship do not involve choosing between two other people, but between putting ourselves first or last in our list of priorities. This choice is obviously one that is resolved by having a good boundary with doors. This is the opposite situation of that for a sensitive or even over-sensitive, irritable person, as shown in the following diagram.

"Thin Skin": Holes in the Boundary

Surely you have had the experience of "walking on eggshells" with a friend. We all have an inner intuition about our friends regarding how sensitive they are at any given time, what their hot-button issues are, and what leads to nurturing respect and a sense of positive emotion. Friends like this have holes in their boundaries (as Jennifer did) and let stress get in too easily. That brings their moods down and therefore brings new *negative* energy into their friendships.

Just as with any issue in friendship, the master checklist applies. We always need to remember to be consistent, mutual, sharing, and positive in our emotions with friends if we want to grow closer and have higher quality connections with others. It was time for Tina to learn to use very diplomatic boundary skills and time for Jennifer to learn to use boundary muscles on the only person she had not learned to use them on—herself.

Remember, we do not control the uncontrollable. Trying to do so creates suffering. Jennifer was causing this for both herself and Tina. She was burning their emotional energy on something that could not be eradicated by magic: her husband leaving her and her illness. Suffering always happens through our boundary holes.

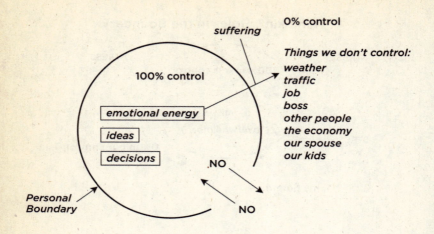

The Effect of Boundary "Holes" with Stress

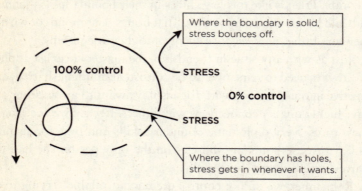

You end up having a good day only because the environment is good and you always have a "bad" day when the environment is "bad."

This means the uncontrollable has total control of you. This is not good.

Boundary holes also let stress into our lives too easily, which was certainly happening to Jennifer.

Where there are boundary holes, there is irritability to your mood. You end up having a good day only because the environment is good and a bad day whenever the environment is bad. This means that the uncontrollable in life has total control of you, which is obviously not a good place to be.

When we are being oversensitive, we are simply in a situation where our boundary is exceptionally weak. It is full of holes or diminished in its resiliency for protecting us from stress. Sometimes a mature person with a solid boundary with good doors lives under stress for so long, or receives such a large amount of stress, that the boundary wears down. This person becomes more "thin-skinned" for a time, and is considered to have suffered a regression, a step back in the maturity of their character.

Stress, if it gets in through a thin, weak, or hole-filled boundary, lowers our self-esteem:

Stress and Self-esteem

0% control

100% control

stress
(negative energy)

self-esteem
(positive energy)

personal boundary

As we can see, the positive energy that friendship is dependent on is self-esteem, and this energy lowers with every ounce of stress we let ourselves absorb. It is helpful to remember that stress is part hurt and part loss. If we divide up our stresses this way and write

Stress = Hurt + Loss

in a journal about them, we get a handle on them by unearthing new details: hurt causes anger if it gets into us by lowering our well-being, and loss causes anxiety if it gets into us by lowering our confidence.

In fact, another way of looking at this is that if the stress called *hurt* gets into us, it causes *anger*, and that anger is simply a decrease in feeling the type of self-esteem called *well-being*:

Stress and Self-esteem

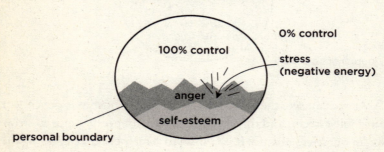

Remember two important equations here:

Stress = Hurt + Loss

and

Self-esteem = Well-being + Confidence

Stress and self-esteem are opposites. Stress is the negative energy that brings down friendships and self-esteem is the lifeblood of friendships, the very positive energy at its core.

In a UCLA study on the connection between stress-relief and friendship, Gale Berkowitz writes:

The discovery that women respond to stress differently than men was made in a classic "aha" moment shared by two women scientists who were talking one day in a lab at UCLA. There was this joke that when the women who worked in the lab were stressed, they came in, cleaned the lab, had coffee, and bonded, says Dr. Klein. When the men were stressed, they holed up somewhere on their own. I commented one day to fellow researcher Shelley Taylor that nearly 90% of the stress research is on males. I showed her the data from my lab, and the two of us knew instantly that we were onto something.

It may take some time for new studies to reveal all the ways that oxytocin encourages us to care for children and hang out with other women, but the "tend and befriend" notion developed by Drs. Klein and Taylor may explain why women consistently outlive men. Study after study has found that social ties reduce our risk of disease by lowering blood pressure, heart rate, and cholesterol. There's no doubt, says Dr. Klein, that friends are helping us live longer.

So friendship has direct impact on our very mortality. The unique ways in which women connect offer much for us to learn from in terms of our survival. Stress is the mediator between the negative energy of the social world and the inner world of physiology, disease, and mortality.

When we combine the definition of self-esteem with the definition of stress, we have a complete method of transforming the negative energy of stress in our lives to the positive, friendship-building energy of self-esteem. Just return to the Anger Map and Anxiety Map to see how to transform your stress into self-esteem and therefore friendship growth.

If we look at the exact way these equations play out in diagram form, we start to turn all that is invisible about psychology into a visible and powerful way to solve problems.

Relationship of Stress and Self-esteem

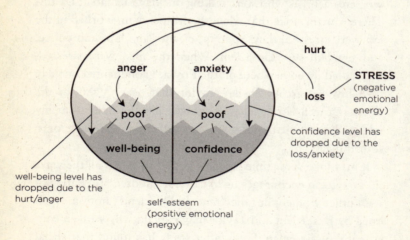

What has happened here is that any kind of stress that comes into your life (like Jennifer's lupus flare-up or separation or Tina's work challenges) can get into your boundary in one of two ways. Either you are not very mature and have holes in your boundary, or the stress itself is so overwhelming (as perhaps in Jennifer's case) that it busts through your boundary anyway.

Since we know that stress is part hurt and part loss, and stress is simply negative emotional energy, those two parts then diminish the corresponding parts of positive emotional energy, well-being and confidence, which together form self-esteem. In this diagram, you clearly see all the possible ways that we can be stressed and how stress affects the basic elements of our self-esteem.

For Jennifer, the dilemma was whether to choose her own health over the way she appeared to her friends, especially the new single ones. She wanted to look fun and free, able to party, smoke, and capture the attention of men. This was driven by her feminine need for belonging and feeling "normal," the need to be accepted by a circle of friends with something in common with her. Yet this was doomed to failure if she ignored the core importance of using her boundary to respect herself: by saying no to many of their demands to be that fun party girl, by saying no to her own tendency to do self-destructive things like partying (out of the reptilian impulse to belong), and by dividing up and budgeting her energy so that she can be responsible to her children and her potential employer.

For Jennifer, there was indeed stress: the *loss* of her husband, the *hurt* of his leaving, the *loss* of health and companionship. In this state, she didn't make a very good friend to Tina or anyone else. Jennifer thought Tina was being insensitive when in fact Jennifer was tearing away at the quality of her friendship with Tina by refusing to take good care of herself and remaining in a negative emotional state. Tina was behaving as any normal, mature person would in trying to be supportive while still trying to keep her own mood (and therefore self-esteem) healthy.

Many women get into a situation where their reptilian brain's gender-based instincts lead them to deep intimacy with a friend, and they then feel even more feminine and full of identity as a woman for being so caring and maternal to others. However, what if this friend is chronically down, refuses to help herself, or is highly irritable and tries to latch on to your already career-drained energy? In this case, you feel "crowded" or "overwhelmed" with the friend's neediness. This was happening to Tina, and part of her way of dealing with it without feeling herself to be less feminine was to use bluntness and quick solutions as a defense against Jennifer's overwhelming problems.

As you can see, all the stress in Jennifer's life can be categorized as hurts or losses, and they added up to equal all the threats to her self-esteem level, her "sense of self." Yet being able to categorize the two types of stress and two types of self-esteem gives us power to deal with dilemmas and mood problems like this in a very practical, step-by-step way, with help from the Anger Map and Anxiety Map. Jennifer only needs to label each hurt, figure out how it is derived from a need going unmet, then use assertiveness to go out and fill the need herself. Likewise, for every loss and fear she has (such as falling ill with lupus), she needs to face that fear or loss with courage, to find new confidence in herself.

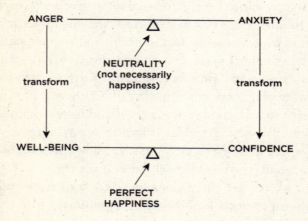

Together, the new well-being she gets from getting her needs met and the new confidence she gets from courageously facing her fears will replenish her total self-esteem. She, and all of us, can literally transform stress into self-esteem, which is the lifeblood of friendship and the source of all happiness and success in our lives.

As a kind friend, Tina's path to getting Jennifer there, though, involved contending with Jennifer's weakened boundary, and the overwhelming nature of Jennifer's various stresses would have weakened even one with great fortitude.

In fact, any time we use the word *overwhelm* or any vague word to describe mood situations, dilemmas, or challenges—phrases like "I kind of don't know how I feel" or "I feel empty" or "my plate's too full" or "I'm confused"—it means there is a boundary problem. The very notion that our "plate is too full" means that there are holes in our boundary and we are leaking self-esteem out of them. The plate *is* the boundary.

"Thin Skin": Holes in the Boundary

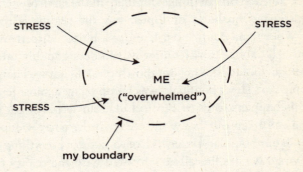

"Thin skin" refers to a thinning of the boundary. When we have "buttons" that people push, they are holes in the boundary.

"Thin Skin": Holes in the Boundary

When we say we're overwhelmed, or use any vague emotional expression, it means we have holes in our boundary.

As you see above, we do not control what we do not control, but for those in dilemmas like Jennifer's, it can appear that we do. Imagine looking out one of those holes. You would not see the limit of what you own and control in life. It would seem like you *should* be able to control things out there in the environment, such as an estranged husband or lupus, but the reality is that you cannot. When Tina confronted Jennifer a bit too directly and undiplomatically about this, Jennifer was understandably infuriated (from her viewpoint, looking out those holes). What was happening was simply that Tina's boundary was bumping up against Jennifer's. When this happens to us, it can feel like our left arm got up and walked away from our body. In other words, when we look out the holes in our boundary, it *seems* like we control everything around us. But when we are literally confronted with the reality that we do not control much of our daily lives, it is threatening and scary. In reality, you never *did* control things like estranged husbands, major medical illnesses, the job market, or anything else beyond your boundary, your self-esteem, and your decisions about both.

This is why I say that people with boundary holes are *irritable*, and irritable people most certainly have lots of boundary holes. This is a special secret psychology clue to the deep inner workings of people's psychology.

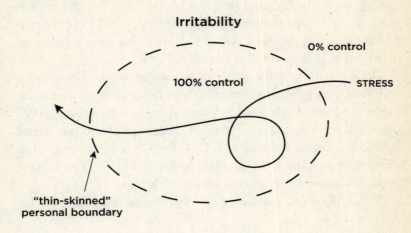

With a person like this in your life, you could very well be blunt, like Tina, but chances are the friend is going to run away from you and not like you anymore. Politics is necessary, and what this friendship dilemma produced for both Tina and Jennifer was a chance to learn where each other's boundaries were and how to be diplomatic in the face of stress. Diplomacy is a great, great power in friendship. And it too has an equation by which it works:

Politics = Decisions + Boundary function (with the Cool Eye on)

Now, for the first time, you can literally see politics. It is the combined use of our boundaries and our decisions. When we have doors in our boundary, we can budget our resources wisely, like Hestia. We can use just the right amount of love at the right time, in the right way (which of course is also guided by our Cool Eye) that gets our friends to understand us and to work with us to do the right thing.

As you might deduce, all three of these elements—the Cool Eye, decision making, and personal boundary skills—are higher-brain skills. We know that friends we consider cool have the self-observing ability of the Cool Eye. Notice that people who are masterful at politics are also considered cool.

Doesn't it then make sense, in friendship or any other social endeavor, that gifted politics consists of being cool, wise, and capable of multiple relationships, some of which have doors wide open to advantageous situations and nearly or completely closed to disadvantageous situations? This is what our boundary-door diagram shows and what Tina had to develop in order to assist in Jennifer's dilemma of "friends versus her health."

This is the secret psychological key to masterful politics:

Semi-permeable Boundary with "Doors," Not "Holes"

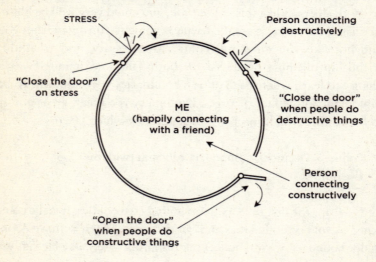

We learned earlier that someone without doors in their boundary—someone with holes only, for example—is incapable of commitment. With a dominance of boundary holes, a friend of yours is insecure, weak, irritable, overwhelmed, breaks promises, and tends not to budget very well. They waste their time, energy, and money as well as yours. They always say yes when they mean no and can't take no for an answer very well. This person is a bad politician. This person will tend to embarrass you at parties, in the workplace, and in circles of friends. Her friendships tend to be codependent, and she can make you that way as well. You need to stay at the acquaintance level with people like this in order to be a good friendship politician.

What about people dominated by walls in their boundaries? Friends like this tend to say no to everything you request of them or invite them to. They waste your time, energy, and money as you try to reach them. You find yourself banging your head against their boundary as you "try to get through to them." Many women tend to complain that men behave this way with them. These people might be said to be overly independent, set apart from most social groups, and can be called loners. Do they make good politicians of friendship? No. Keep them as acquaintances, too, if you are to be a masterful friendship politician.

Only friends with decision-making wisdom coupled with a nice set of boundary doors can have the diplomacy to weather miscommunications, misunderstandings, and mutual outside stress the way Tina eventually learned to do in her friendships. You can learn to open your doors to mutually useful, win-win deals with those around you, and close those doors for a time with friends who keep offering you emotionally draining, win-lose deals the way Jennifer offered Tina.

Have you ever had a friend be unforgiving of you long after you had done everything in your power to learn from your mistakes and make amends? Did you have a vague intuition that this person was somehow childish in doing so? Now you know why. You have more of a Seventh Sense of people: an immediate gut feeling as to what is going on and the psychological mathematics of *why*. You might then say that immature people make poor politicians and mature people make good ones—true leaders. The cure for the immaturity of unforgivingness is simply the discipline to learn to open doors in your boundary: to shut out intimacy where your boundary meets a friend's closed or weak boundary, while being willing in the future to open up that door again if the friend proves to have grown into more mature, win-win, constructive dealings with you.

This is a special feature of friendship, just as it was for Tina and Jennifer. When we are only friends for survival reasons (of the type you might see in a high school's social jungle), it is because the mere association with others protects us and gives us a sense of belonging. On the other end of the spectrum, where we are deeply committed to each other, as by contract, such as roommates or in a marriage, our boundaries have actually joined a bit to create a shared reality. Yet in friendship (where there is no legal or implied commitment), boundaries only abut each other, pointing out to us the strengths of

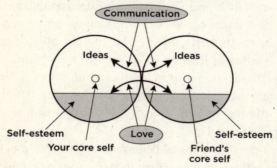

Whether through a hole or a door, and therefore regardless of maturity level, love and communication happen at the "EDGE" of two people's adjoining personal boundaries.

our character and the weaknesses or holes in our boundary. The boundaries of friendship align right next to each other as such:

In this form, our friends are perfectly situated to neither overly invade our space nor be so distant as to not truly know us. All acts of love and understanding through communication occur at that remarkable interface where the boundaries touch.

Take the master checklist and look at the friendship between Tina and Jennifer. Jennifer's dilemma was about deciding between treating herself well and keeping a sense of belonging with new friends. Tina's dilemma was between being herself (with her blunt way of talking) versus taking the risk of losing or offending a friend. In the end, it was not necessary to choose. You don't need to choose between two very important options when you have great diplomatic skills and a mature set of boundary doors. The way this played out in the core of their friendship was that they had a long period of *consistent, good emotion* between them, and things were usually *mutual*. They *shared* intimately about their lives for many years, with good communication. However, Jennifer's recent loss of a husband and a degree of physical ill health threw their friendship off kilter in the mutuality and sharing departments. Only the development of good political skill could weather this new stress to their system and set the mutuality and sharing back on the right course.

The same is true for you.

The Dilemma Checklist

- Go over your master checklist.

- Friends vs. family: Do you have an ability to join circles of friends together or even to include friends in family activities? If not, make a circle-triangle diagram to look at the dynamics and see what you can do.

- Friends vs. a man: Do you have enough of a reserve of self-esteem to value your own feminine sense of belonging with friends as something to balance with time and energy spent on your man?

- Friends vs. work: Do you focus on positive energy? Do you know how to transform negative energy to positive? If not, go to the Anger Map and Anxiety Map. Do you know how to use boundary triangles to evaluate the nature of your friendships' positive or negative energy in the workplace versus your private life? Review the use of boundaries.

- Friends vs. your health (or yourself): Do you sometimes take your own health or self for granted? Do you sometimes trade treating yourself wrongly or irresponsibly in exchange for a sense of belonging? Maybe it is time to back up and learn that politics enables you to balance what is good for you against keeping out what is bad for you. In the end, your feminine reptilian brain will appreciate belonging to a circle of friends who would want you to treat yourself, and your health, first.

Chapter Nine

Long-distance Friendships

More than kisses, letters mingle souls,
For thus, friends absent speak.
—JOHN DONNE

WHEN SHE *heard the sound that her computer made upon re-*
ceiving new e-mail, Samantha paid it little attention. It was prob-
ably just spam, something she'd been getting more of lately. What
had once seemed like a great tool for staying in touch with the
people who mattered to her had become just another vehicle for
advertising and worse. Therefore, Samantha didn't check her e-
mail for nearly a half hour—and when she did, it sent her hurtling
into the past.

I've just landed back on planet Earth and I'm looking for the
shelter of old friends.

Bella had a new e-mail address—Samantha knew the old one
by heart—and she was finally, finally, getting back in touch. Im-
mediately, the face of Samantha's dear old friend rose up in front
of her. The bright eyes, the thousand-watt smile. And with that vi-
sion, Samantha missed her terribly, more terribly than she ever
had before. It was as though all of the time and distance between
them swept upon her in one huge gust.

Samantha never could have imagined going this long without contact with Bella. They'd turned long-distance friendship into an art form. After all, they'd been friends for nearly twenty years, and yet they'd only lived in the same town for one of those years. They met as interns on Face-to-Face, *the hit Indianapolis talk show that launched the career of one of America's biggest media stars. The pace was insane, and Samantha and Bella loved it. They'd decompress together afterward at a local restaurant or bar, often skipping out on sleep because they had too much to say to each other or too many laughs to share. The end of the one-year stint sent them to opposite coasts, but never away from each other. Nearly every month one found a "business" excuse to visit the other, and they spent at least forty-five minutes on the phone with each other nearly every day, offering elaborate details of everything that was happening in their lives. Really, they couldn't have been closer if they were roommates.*

Then the slide happened. Samantha thought back to her wedding weekend, now five years ago. She was so happy to be marrying Larry and nearly as thrilled that Bella was going to be her maid of honor and had agreed to spend the entire week leading up to the wedding with her. But when Bella showed up, Samantha could tell that something was a little off. She could read it in Bella's face and actions, even though she couldn't glean anything from Bella's words. At the altar, Bella sobbed. However, her tears didn't seem like the tears of joy so often shed at weddings. Bella seemed genuinely sad.

It would be weeks before Samantha learned what was going on. It turned out that Tom, Bella's fiancé, had been cheating on her and she was so distraught that she couldn't even tell her best friend.

"Bella, get your ass on the next plane to New York," Samantha said when she finally found out. "We need an all-nighter together."

"I can't," Bella said forlornly. "You have Larry and—"

"Larry will be fine with this. Really, get on a plane."

"I can't. Soon, maybe."

But "soon" never came. Bella became increasingly morose during their phone conversations and her e-mail messages were terse. Samantha offered to come out to L.A. so the two of them could spend some quality time together, but Bella always had a reason why it wasn't a good moment. After a while, Samantha stopped offering. As guilty as she felt about it, she had to acknowledge that Bella had become a serious buzz kill. Nearly all communication with her left Samantha feeling drained and depressed. The phone calls, e-mail, and texting slowed dramatically and eventually stopped, and Samantha let it happen without a fight. After twenty years, it appeared that their friendship had run its course, leaving Samantha feeling powerless and terribly sad.

I've been thinking about you a lot lately. I miss you and I really miss what we had together. I've never had another friend like you, and I think I've figured a lot of things out. Life looks a whole lot better these days.

One of the things I've figured out is that an all-night bull session with you in the near future would be a dream come true. If you have any interest, give me a call at (310) 555–6732.

Samantha nearly cried reading the words. She grabbed her phone and quickly dialed the number. When Bella answered, Samantha had one thing to say to her:

"Bella, get your ass on the next plane to New York."

Bella laughed—a big belly laugh Samantha had nearly forgotten. Then Bella said softly, "I was hoping so much you'd say that."

The Connection Dilemma

I have seen hundreds of cases of romantic couples newly challenged with long-distance problems. Men and women geographically separate, then struggle to keep their relationships intact. They receive cannot-refuse job offers out of state, but the spouse or significant other needs to remain behind for a number of months. The desperate engagement, the promises to stay true, and the flood of communication that at first feeds the ongoing fires of love eventually wanes to a trickle and dies. In my professional experience, most cases of long-distance romance do not end well and there is a scientific reason why: there must be friendship in every romance or the sexuality, commitment, and everything else will soon fail.

Long-distance friendships stand a better chance, though. Without the expectations and strings attached of a sexual connection or a formal commitment, friendship is free to be as flexible as our lives need to be today.

Long-distance friendships suffer in the extreme from something that affects all of our friendships: lack of connection. If we look at it from an evolutionary perspective, setting human development side by side with the advance of communication technology, we see the dramatic challenge with regard to our ability to adapt to changing needs for communication and human connectedness.

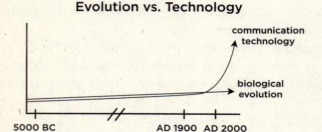

Evolution vs. Technology

For thousands or even millions of years, we have evolved more slowly than glaciers do. Yet our ability to create new forms of technology has exploded in the past hundred years. This has created something of a crisis for face-to-face interaction.

There are great advantages to our technological progress. After all, we can do more, quicker and on a larger scale, but in the case of communication, we can't do it *better*. Perhaps in another million years the equivalent of a cell phone will be an anatomic part of our brains, and a wireless Internet antenna will sprout from our noses. Whether this is good or bad I cannot say, but one thing is certain: we are social animals and simply not biologically equipped to maintain our emotional lifelines exclusively by silicon circuits and radio transmitters.

Anthropologist Dr. Paul Ekman's work centered for decades on the incredibly interesting and complex ways that humans communicate emotional meaning through their facial muscles. After studying many thousands of videotapes of individuals from cultures around the world, Ekman concluded that human communication amounts to roughly 97 percent nonverbal cues, largely in micromovements of the dozens of muscles in the human face.

The most complicated written language on earth is Chinese, with more than one thousand characters. However, Ekman found that the human face can communicate in more than eight thousand "syllables" or "characters," all of which produce an emotional meaning for those of us on the receiving end, and one that is largely the same across all cultures and spoken languages. This is remarkable; it means that there is a universal language of the human face that crosses all borders. And it has been this way since the time of the cavemen.

If you go back to the master checklist, you'll easily see the friendship characteristic most affected by distance. It is *sharing*. Remember, if *any* of the characteristics are absent, it is easy for the other three to gradually decay and kill the friendship. In the case of absent sharing, it is easy for us to have a gradual differing of worldviews, a growing apart, which is a boundary phenomenon since our boundary houses our worldview or set of belief systems. Alongside this, when we do not have much sharing and comparing of notes on our experiences, it is easier for the holes that inevitably remain in our ever-maturing boundaries to foster projection, that process of projecting out onto the blank screen of another less-known person those aspects of our own sense of self that we find "bad" or "wrong." Distance then makes it easy for our imaginations to run wild, for us to assume ill intent in the friend who did not call us at the appointed time, maybe even on our birthday.

In this unconscious social strategy projection, you take the feelings of "badness" inside and attribute them to someone else, such as a friend or coworker who already has her boundary open to you in some intimacy. Then you temporarily feel better about yourself, claiming only the remaining goodness you also have inside. Projection is the cause of all scapegoating, gossip, and slander in our social systems.

When an angry person projects, it is as if she is seeing—through a hole in her boundary—anger in a friend that is really inside herself. Eventually, the insistence that the friend is angry may in fact

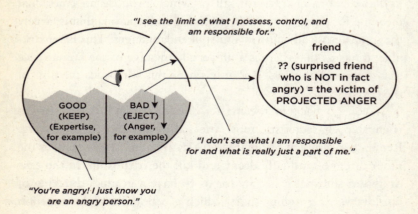

anger that friend, and a self-fulfilling prophecy occurs. We unconsciously find a way to make our desires come true through this invisible social effect. A very real "dumping" of our anger on to another person has occurred.

In 1992, a new kind of neuron was discovered called a "mirror neuron." In essence, what these neurons allow us to do is to put ourselves in the shoes of others. When a friend tells us a tale of happiness or sadness from her life—if we are in the present moment, using our Cool Eye to pay attention—we literally feel and experience what *she* is feeling and experiencing, as if it had happened to *us*. Distance makes this tougher. If our friends use e-mail, text, and the phone to communicate to us, they need remarkable skill to approximate the power of telling a story in person. For most of us, there is no substitute for the vivid experience of hearing a friend's story face-to-face—with the accompanying tears, smiles, and range of meaning in the muscles of the face and body.

The greater the physical distance and time apart, the more our brains naturally fill a need for a coherent story to our lives. Try this example: draw a solid circle on a sheet of paper. What is it called? A circle of course. Then draw another circle next to it using a dotted line instead. What is *that* shape called? A circle? No. A circle is a solid line in the shape of a ring. What you have drawn second is not a circle, but a series of dashes with spaces between them. It is our brain's need for completion, for filling in gaps, that causes us to errantly call the second drawing a circle. As you can see from the above diagram of projection, the assumptions we make that our long-distance friends no longer like us, are angry at us, or are punishing us are in reality negative views or beliefs that come from our view of *ourselves*. We are the ones who don't like ourselves right now, who are angry, and feel like punishing ourselves or others. This is what Bella was doing to, and assuming of, Samantha. The way we make assumptions about a long-distance friend, then, is far less an objective view of the reality of what that friend is thinking than it is of how we view ourselves.

The very same boundary effects of interpersonal distance affect our tendency to *lie*. We can only learn interpersonal boundaries by bumping our hole-ridden boundaries up against theirs and encountering the word *no*—to have differences of opinion and thereby to learn where our limits are and those of others begin. For eons in our evolution, up until only recently, when we hurt others or caused them loss, the lessons we learned from those run-ins would inform our consciences face-to-face.

Likewise, the consequences of unethical behavior would be met with physical confrontation or disapproval from the physical community of others surrounding us. Have you ever heard of an alcoholic "intervention" performed through a mass e-mail as opposed to in-person? I haven't, either, and it would not be effective. The physical consequences of unethical behavior shaped the

Lies and Boundary Holes

A lie is used as a smokescreen to cover a "hole" in the personal boundary instead of saying NO to the person directly regarding a request for access to your thoughts and emotions.

Observer who thinks she has real access to the person's inner thoughts and identity.

evolution of our consciences, our sense of ethics. Without the in-person effect of sharing in friendship, there are no immediate consequences of such behaviors as lying, no penalty within the circle of friends as long as the physically isolated friend is free to make up her own inner, personal worldview unencumbered by the corrective view of others.

It serves us well, then, to assume the best of people, not because this is absolute objective reality, but because it encourages us to be in an emotional state that benefits us in our actions and in our friendships. If we apply the Golden Rule, we more often than not will receive the reciprocal altruism hardwired into the human mind. To be mutual in a friendship is to receive back automatically. If not, you need to use the personal boundary to put a stop to the interaction. Yet the relationship can't be mutual if you are not even sharing in the first place.

What is a worldview and how does it affect long-distance relationships? What does one's worldview (or belief systems) have to do with our communications within friendships?

Our diagram of a belief shows that we are exposed to all kinds of ideas on a daily basis, some positive and beneficial to us and some negative. The worldview we hold, or set of beliefs we already have, causes us to filter or selectively snatch up those random ideas drifting around us, incorporating them into our view of ourselves and the world as new evidence for those same views. For the same reasons, adaptive biases that in rare cases are still able to save our lives (which is why they evolved)—conclusions like "where there's smoke, there's fire"—are why we need our beliefs to filter reality for us. Just as a dotted line can make us think *circle*, we need the story-gap-filling ability of our brains to keep us functional in a world where there is never total certainty, never total proof and explanation of what is going on around us. We are actually walking bags of hunches. We *have to* be or we would be relegated to calculating every probability and possibility of the

Beliefs Are Like a Tabletop: Supported by Legs Called "Evidence"

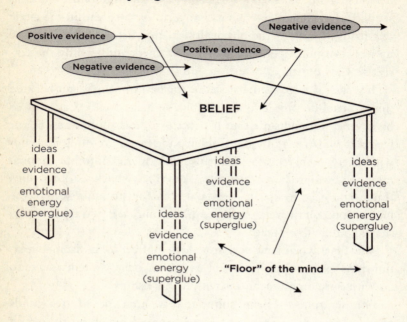

outcome of our next footstep on a walk in the park. Nowhere is this a more confusing, uncertain predicament than in the social world of friendship.

The Communication Equation

When we are far from friends, our communication is impaired, even with electronic means of being in touch. There is no substitute for face-to-face interaction because that is how our brains evolved for millions of years.

That said, there is much you can do with the power of empathy and being present-minded when you communicate with a long-distance friend. Remember that best friends have great boundaries with each other and they are consistent, mutual, and have positive emotion to give each other even if their face-to-face sharing is limited. Be aware of how projection happens, how lies are easy, and how negative emotion is a friendship killer. To slow down and be aware of all this—giving extra attention to the importance of present-minded communication—requires you to have your Cool Eye turned on.

Communication has an equation all its own. Whether we use words as speech or text (3 percent of communication) or use the muscles of the face in person (97 percent of communication), we are sending more than just ideas to another person. We are sending emotional energy. Communication is the actual transmission of our worldview to others, through symbols (like facial expression) and language itself.

Communication = Ideas + Emotional energy

With our new equation, you can see the importance of communication in friendship as more than just a fanciful bit of kitchen-table wisdom. Our communication to friends carries emotional energy, and we know from the master checklist that friendship is entirely dependent on the presence of positive emotional energy transferred between people.

Do you have your Cool Eye turned on often these days? Do you use it to view how much positive-energy communication you have with your friends versus negative-energy communication? If you are frequently depressed, anxious, angry, bored, annoyed, contentious, or any other negative emotion, are you aware that these emotional states naturally bleed into the energy of your

communications with friends or potential friends—literally causing you to lose friends on a daily basis or to lower the quality of
your friendships?

Character is destiny. Character is manifest in friendships and
grows from them. And communication is the vehicle of the act of
loving that defines friendship. It is very, very important in long-
distance friendships because you don't share face time. For example, to one person, the idea communicated by the word *convertible*
causes her positive emotion because she remembers the time she
lived in California and drove joyfully along the coast in a convertible. Yet to her friend, the idea communicated by *convertible*
causes negative emotion because she remembers the dearly loved ex
who drove a convertible and is now a loss in her life. If a conversation
between these friends brings up the word *convertible*, they may unwittingly proceed into a wide divergence of emotion that makes no
sense to either of them unless they previously shared their feelings
about convertibles. If they had their Cool Eyes turned on, they
would notice the dramatic change in emotional tone of the conversation and one of them would stop and say, "What just happened
here? Did I say something that bothers you?" Or the other might

Communication

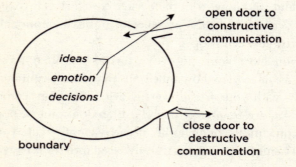

stop and say, "Wow, sorry. You just reminded me of my ex."

While comparing notes on our beliefs and worldviews seems like common sense to most of us, we rarely actively do it in everyday life, least of all in long-distance friendships. Why? Because the normal social cues in the face and body are absent when we e-mail, text, or use the phone. It then becomes even more important to remember to purposely compare notes, to color our language with emotion, to recognize the necessary lack of sharing alongside each other that comes with long-distance friendship and to account for the divergence of personal experience during the time you spend apart.

One of the most difficult things to realize when we lack boundary skill or the Cool Eye to look at our boundaries is that we all have different ideas, beliefs that have attached emotion to the ideas, and worldviews composed of all those thousands of beliefs clustered together within our boundary, locked to the floor of the mind by emotion. When we differ in opinion, we have every right to hold to our worldview, but the distance between friends makes the difference of opinion difficult to mend through shared experience.

People like people who share their beliefs, whether positive or negative in emotional nature. Obviously, friendships formed over gossip and complaining about all that is bad in the world tend to not last very long, while those that develop from *liking* each other, based on similar positive emotional beliefs, thrive. In the end, whether living near and sharing experience often or living far away from our friends, one of the crucial communication skills we can learn is how to find a compromise that we *share*. This engenders liking of each other and is the closest substitute to physically shared experience because it drills to the root base of our beliefs.

When we are physically distant, the cure is to find common beliefs and ideas. These take us into the inner sense of personal reality that carries positive emotion. Long-distance bickering can be far more destructive to a friendship. Turning on your Cool Eyes

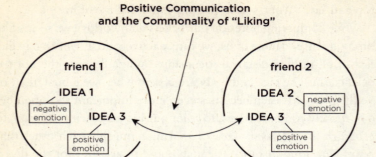

together, being aware of how you communicate, project, tend to lie, and diverge in your opinions can lead you to purposely nurture those things you've always had and likely will always have in common. The good emotions of friendship will arise naturally in two friends who make the effort, even over long distance.

Let's look again at the story that began this chapter. Bella took some time off from communicating with her friend until she got her romantic and career lives together, after which she had more positive emotions and beliefs about herself to share. This jelled well with Samantha's need to share her own ongoing successes and positive feelings. Love could then begin again with their careful return to communicating over the three thousand miles that never really harmed what they shared in the past. Only now, their friendship has become even richer than ever. The falling out was only another lesson of life.

In all friendship situations, we grow from acquaintance toward best friendship. The more we move out of the survival mode of the reptilian brain into the emotions of the mammalian brain, converting the negatives to positives, then on into the communication, consistency, sharing, and mutuality of the higher brain, our character improves and so does our friendship.

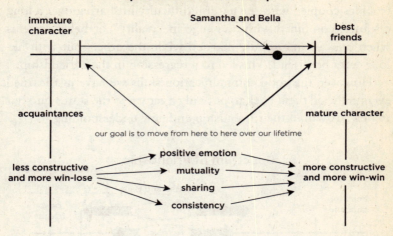

Spectrum of Friendship

immature character — Samantha and Bella — best friends

acquaintances — mature character

our goal is to move from here to here over our lifetime

less constructive and more win-lose →
- positive emotion
- mutuality
- sharing
- consistency
→ more constructive and more win-win

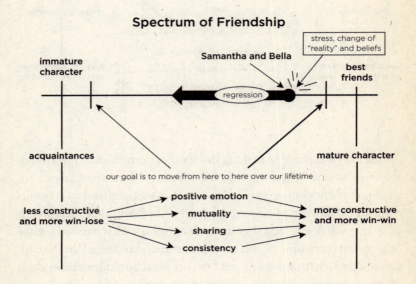

Spectrum of Friendship

immature character

stress, change of "reality" and beliefs

Samantha and Bella — best friends

regression

acquaintances — mature character

our goal is to move from here to here over our lifetime

less constructive and more win-lose →
- positive emotion
- mutuality
- sharing
- consistency
→ more constructive and more win-win

What happened with Samantha and Bella was that Bella's troubles coupled with the natural difficulty in sharing over a long distance, combined with a change in "reality" or belief systems when one became solidly married while the other split with her long-term boyfriend. This led to a regression in their friendship.

However, the good communication skills we have just learned eventually led them back to not only a return to the status quo but to new growth in their friendship and new understanding.

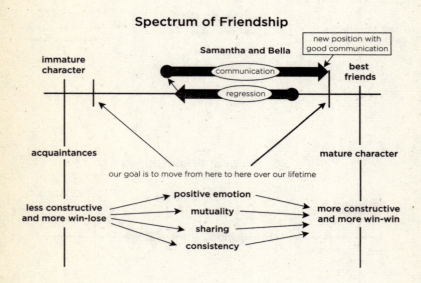

Spectrum of Friendship

We are all capable of making this kind of correction to our friendship regressions. When we form friendships, we are a system of two, a team that doesn't necessarily have an enormous agreed-to commitment to each other. However, the kind of bonding that comes with deep teamwork and best friendship does bring with it a natural sense of growing commitment (because of mature boundaries). In the end, this ability to turn things around makes great communication skills among our most powerful tools in the fix-it box of friendship.

The Long-distance Checklist

- Do you have your Cool Eye turned on? If not, turn it on!

- Remember the master checklist: Consistent, mutual, shared positive emotion. The biggest challenge with distance is usually the sharing part.

- Can you find ways to spend some time physically together from time to time?

- Do you harbor negative beliefs that carry with them negative emotional energy? If so, be aware that when you communicate only by text, e-mail, or phone, the negative energy may be transmitted without much emotional explanation, and the mere words can be misunderstood, projected onto, and not necessarily be as honest as they can be.

- Use your Cool Eye to scan for negativity you actually harbor toward yourself projecting onto your long-distance friends. Turn it around by honest communication with yourself and your friends. Do something to change your own negativity. (Hint: go to the Anger and Anxiety maps.)

- Use your Cool Eye to scan for disagreements of opinion. Instead of hovering over these disagreements, find a compromise, an opinion you both share. Enjoy the good emotion that comes with this and use it to reintroduce your differences of opinion at some point later on, with increased mutual understanding.

- When physical togetherness and sharing is not possible, remember the power of sharing positive energy beliefs you have about yourselves and life. These can take the place of physically shared experience, for now, because all of our beliefs clustered together are what make our "reality" anyway.

Chapter Ten

Toxic Friendships

Treat people as if they were what they ought to be, and you help them to become what they are capable of being.

— J. W. VON GOETHE

FRIENDSHIP IS the only beast that's never known to bite until it's dead." Lisa remembered hearing that line in a song once, though she couldn't remember the song itself. It had never meant as much to her as it did today.

She'd called Kelly a few minutes ago to ask her to come to her office. Since then, Lisa's stomach had been roiling. She was so much better now at facing difficult tasks than she ever was before, but she still felt a twinge in her gut when she had to confront someone. In reality, that was probably a good thing. It kept her from being needlessly aggressive, something Lisa always disliked in others.

It was hard to believe it had come to this. Lisa and Kelly had become fast friends a year and a half ago after they met at a convention. Kelly was funny and incredibly clever, and she seemed to want the same things from life that Lisa wanted. This felt especially good to Lisa because she was coming out of an intense period of growing pains. She'd split with her longtime best friend when she lost a considerable amount of weight and discovered that Renee only liked having her around because she played the role of "ugly sidekick." On top of this, Lisa and her boyfriend called it quits, which led her into a deep funk that somehow caused several of her other friends to walk away from her. It took a while for Lisa to realize that she'd become too needy and to understand that extreme neediness and friendship weren't good partners. By the time she met Kelly, Lisa felt as though she'd grown up enormously.

Her friendship with Kelly paid instant benefits when Kelly tipped her off to a great job and then went out of her way to sell Lisa to her new employers. Kelly was amazing, really. From what Lisa heard, she made management feel as though they'd regret it the rest of their lives if they didn't hire Lisa.

"You're almost as good as advertised," her boss said three months ago when he promoted her.

"What do you mean?"

"Well, you know, Kelly was so over the top about you that we started to wonder a little. She made you sound like a superstar. Of course, we didn't believe anyone could be that good, and we assumed Kelly was just pushing this hard because of the recruitment bonus, but your résumé was great and you interviewed well. As it turns out, all of Kelly's hype was dead-on."

Lisa barely heard the end of what her boss said to her. Her mind stuck on the phrase "recruitment bonus." What was her boss talking about? As it turned out, Kelly received $2,000 for bringing Lisa to the company. This was fine, especially since Lisa was the perfect person for the job, but at the same time Kelly was selling the company on Lisa, she was selling Lisa on the company. Again, this was fine because Lisa liked working there, but now that she thought back on the way Kelly sold her, it became clear that she was doing it for the money, not out of friendship. In fact, when Lisa had a minor misunderstanding with one of the executives a month into the new job, Kelly's response was, "Management around here stinks." At the time, Lisa thought

Kelly was just being supportive. But now she saw it differently—Kelly was pushing her to join a company that Kelly believed was terribly managed just so she could collect some cash.

A couple of nights later, when they were out to dinner, Lisa asked Kelly about the bonus.

"Oh yeah, I got a few bucks for bringing you in. I guess everyone turned out to be a winner, huh?"

Lisa leaned forward in her seat. "Kelly, why did you think this would be a good spot for me?"

Kelly's eyes darted sideways. "Well, it is a good spot for you, right? You've already gotten promoted."

Lisa nodded slowly. "Yes, it is a good spot for me. But you've been complaining endlessly about management since I got here. Why'd you think I'd like it?"

Kelly threw up her hands. "Why are you giving me the third degree about this? You scored big here. What difference does it make if I got a lousy check for hooking you up?"

Lisa might have been content to leave things be if not for what followed. Kelly, obviously feeling threatened by Lisa's suspicions, started gossiping about her to several people on the staff, including her bosses. Kelly clearly didn't think Lisa would hear about this, even though Lisa was now her direct supervisor, because she acted in the same way with Lisa that she always had when they were alone. This came to a head two days earlier when Kelly lied that Lisa was planning to downsize the department, causing several people to rush into Lisa's office to plead a case for their jobs. Kelly had become a cancer, not just in Lisa's life, but in the company as well. And Lisa had to do something about it.

"Hey, what's up," Kelly said, popping her head into Lisa's office.

"Close the door and sit down," Lisa said firmly.

Kelly did so, looking at Lisa darkly as she sat.

"I'm not going to mince words," Lisa said. "You've become a liability to the department and I'm letting you go."

Kelly bolted up in her seat. "What? You can't do this!"

Lisa refused to lose her temper. "I can do it and I am doing it. I have the complete support of upper management."

Kelly's face reddened. "How could you? And you have the nerve to call yourself my friend!"

Lisa took a deep breath. "Actually, I don't. I guess I'm firing you as a friend as well."

The Art of the Girlfriend Divorce

There are deal breakers in friendships. Lying, stealing, mate poaching, public embarrassment, or betrayal of a friend are among the most common. If we begin in the reptilian brain where impulsive, reflexive, passionate responses to the social moves of others stir, we encounter the primal, hardwired instinct in women that promotes strength in togetherness and belonging—and thus the absolute need for *trust*. All of these deal breakers involve broken trust of some sort.

The women who come to see me in treatment tell me that there is a difference between a "girlfriend divorce" (my sister's term) and a "fade-out" or a "drift-apart" in female friendships. In a fade-out, you can "fade back in." The friends who drift apart due to distance, major stresses, changes in life role, and other factors are not necessarily permanently at the end of a friendship. This was not true with Lisa and Kelly because Lisa felt Kelly had done things that went beyond mere temporary, forgivable destructive behavior, into the trust-breaking arena.

Our Cool Eye, our logic, our ethical and intuitive choices, and our boundaries give us the ability to be at the steering wheel of life, in control of our survival reflexes, and to limit the destructiveness of others. The skills we have learned at politics are effective at preventing toxic friendships, their codependence, aggressiveness, passive-aggressiveness, and cause for distrust. Remember our politics equation:

Politics = Decisions + Boundary function (with the Cool Eye on)

Our boundary doors let us distinguish what is constructive (good for us and others) from what is destructive (bad for us, others, or both). Throughout life, those doors absolutely need to be able to open and close or there would be no friends in our lives at all. People are fallible. We make mistakes and need forgiveness for

A Mature Boundary Has Doors, Not Holes or Walls

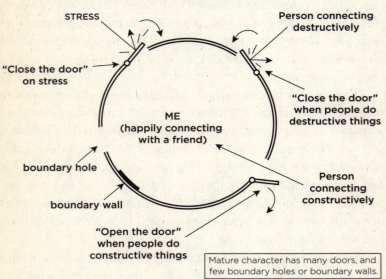

STRESS

Person connecting destructively

"Close the door" on stress

"Close the door" when people do destructive things

ME (happily connecting with a friend)

boundary hole

Person connecting constructively

boundary wall

"Open the door" when people do constructive things

Mature character has many doors, and few boundary holes or boundary walls.

them. When we break trust in little ways, we can repair it by maturing in our character and proving that character on the playing field of friendship. Sometimes, however, we get indications that destructive behavior from a friend will keep coming.

Did you ever notice that when people are unforgiving of little spats it feels somehow creepy or uncomfortable? When people use "the silent treatment," arbitrarily put friends on their "blacklist," or call them names behind their backs, these are all childish ways of using their boundaries to exclude others.

With your Cool Eye turned on, you can notice what makes a friendship toxic and know exactly what to do about it. Toxic friendships are usually between friends who both have immature character (in which case neither is aware of how very toxic the friendship is; we call this codependence) or between friends of extremely mismatched maturity of character. In either of these two situations, there is a lack of Cool Eye to monitor what is happening between them. These friends also have poor boundaries.

In both of the character-maturity comparisons below, but not the one between two mature people with doors in their boundaries, there is significant potential for toxic friendships. This is because of the collection of impaired character traits in the higher brain that come together to make toxicity: lots of holes in the boundary, weakness of conscience or ethics (creating frequent destructive, win-lose behaviors), weak intuition (making a friend naive, quick to allow herself to be used and later resentful), and a tendency to be impaired in using the Cool Eye.

When we mature in a friendship at a rate far different from our friend, sometimes this mismatch causes us to feel like we've become entirely different people from what we used to be. We "grow apart" from our friends. But it is more than that—it is as if we have met a new person for the very first time and are not sure that we really want to be friends with that person. This is okay. We need what we

Relative Maturity and Interdependence vs. Dependence

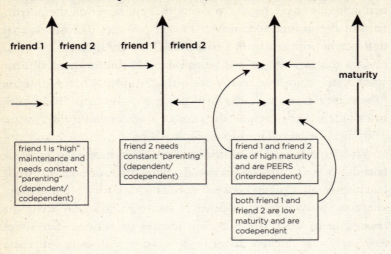

need in life, when we need it. You have no reason to feel guilty about befriending people whose maturity levels are similar to yours and leaving behind those who no longer match you in maturity.

The difference, though, between a "drift apart" or "fade out" and a "girlfriend divorce" is that the latter comes when the gap in maturity between friends is huge and there is a high likelihood of ongoing destructiveness from the friend. With strong boundary consistency, only you know what your limits are, the amount of energy you have, and what your preferences are for tolerating immaturity, lies, betrayal, and broken trust. Only you can decide what is forgivable and what requires mature, respectful severance of the relationship for the good of both of you. Lisa reached this place with Kelly.

Ultimately, the two traits in the master checklist that most often become toxic are the mutuality (it becomes lacking) and positive emotional energy (it turns negative) between friends. The scientific essence of mutuality is win-win behavior—that what benefits one friend benefits both. There is a fair trade of personal resources—time, energy, and ideas—between them, with a boundary solid enough to give us clear preferences and an ability to account for what works for us and what does not. What makes a friendship toxic in terms of mutuality is when there is frequent destructive behavior in the form of many win-lose deals between the friends. The friends use each other in a reptilian-brain "friendship of convenience" and trouble expands from there when a stress hits their system or one friend is more naive and gives too much of herself away while the other is overly shrewd or predatory (top-heavy on intuition and lacking conscience).

In the end, the lack of mutuality in the friendship leads to negative emotions. Someone feels vaguely resentful and does not know why. Another feels put upon or annoyed or "not heard," even though there has been a long history of convenience to the friendship. Of course, if you have your Cool Eye turned on, you can deal with this negative emotion and forgive it before it reaches a point of total betrayal.

Yet if the entire friendship was formed from a misconception, from a misleading pretense of maturity, pretense of respectful boundaries, and a host of lies and deceit, it is good for both people to permanently part ways. This is what Lisa eventually realized with Kelly. For the naive, used friend, this leads to freedom, assertiveness, and growth of better boundary skills. For the shrewd, toxic, codependent user, it provides a potent lesson in conscience, curtailed aggression, and boundaries (which will hopefully lead to growth).

A drift apart does not become a major landmark in a woman's life—it is part of the rise and fall of the tides of friendship. However, the end of a toxic friendship—a girlfriend divorce—can mark a point of growth for a woman. The end of an old chapter and beginning of a new one.

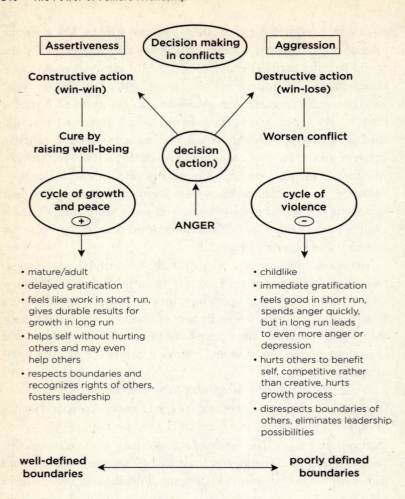

When you are aware of the characteristics that add up to toxicity in friendship, you can assess them in relation to what is destructive versus what is constructive in your life. Your conscience weighs what is destructive in *yourself*, and your intuition can become very good at weighing what you know to be destructive in

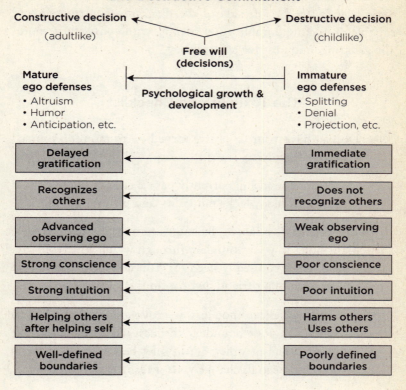

Mature and Constructive vs. Immature and Destructive Commitment

Constructive decision ← ... → Destructive decision

(adultlike)   (childlike)

Free will
(decisions)

Mature ego defenses	Immature ego defenses
• Altruism	• Splitting
• Humor	• Denial
• Anticipation, etc.	• Projection, etc.

Psychological growth & development

Delayed gratification	Immediate gratification
Recognizes others	Does not recognize others
Advanced observing ego	Weak observing ego
Strong conscience	Poor conscience
Strong intuition	Poor intuition
Helping others after helping self	Harms others Uses others
Well-defined boundaries	Poorly defined boundaries

others. This is why using the Cool Eye is the very first step in any human growth or change. You can't change what you don't know exists, so the illustration above is especially useful in helping you identify such things. The right column is essentially a checklist of toxic components of friendship. The left column is a checklist of the basics for best friendship. Lisa and Kelly both used their Cool Eyes poorly at the beginning. Kelly lacked conscience and Lisa lacked intuition. But in the end, Lisa grew from the right side of the diagram above (toxic herself and finding herself surrounded by toxic friends) to the left side of the diagram—constructive and capable of making durable good friends, with consistency, mutuality, sharing, and positive emotion.

The Toxic Friend Checklist

- Do you have your Cool Eye turned on to monitor yourself and your friends?

- Does your friendship currently pass the master checklist? if it is toxic, it likely lacks mutuality and positive emotion.

- Are you passive, naive (lacking intuition), or do you have many holes in your boundary through which you avoid saying no when you really need to? You may need to grow in order to avoid girlfriend divorces in the future.

- Are you aggressive (not just assertive), shrewd, or do you have holes in your boundary through which you cross the rights or limits of others? You may be in for a girlfriend divorce and need to change your ways in order to grow.

- Have you ever stopped to write down the kinds of things that are forgivable in your friendships and can be overcome? If not, you may want to. These will inevitably happen from time to time, and you might decide to instigate a temporary "fade out" of friendship until circumstances change.

- Have you stopped to write down the kinds of things that are utterly unforgivable and invite ongoing disaster if you allow them to stay in your life? These are cause for girlfriend divorce.

- Do you realize that saying good-bye is not a bad thing and doesn't need to be traumatic? Your life will go on and on, and your life belongs to you. If you grow through an experience of girlfriend divorce or a temporary fade out, do you realize that with lessons of life, nothing is wasted? Nothing. It's all right.

- Are you capable of teaching yourself and your friends about boundaries, win-win deals versus win-lose ones, constructiveness and *mature character* versus destructiveness and *immature character*? If so, you are doing everything possible to forgive and heal friendship challenges and to keep toxic friendships from ever getting into your life in the first place.

Chapter Eleven

Best Friendships

Friendship is one soul in two bodies.
—ARISTOTLE

*E*LLEN OPENED *the door to her apartment, dropped her bag on the floor, and then slid to the floor herself. Since she'd arrived in Chicago nearly two years ago, life had been one challenge after another. The winters were so much harsher than they were in Denver. The city was so much bigger; yet with so many people around her, she'd only made a couple of casual friends. And work was killing her.*

Ellen prided herself on her analytical skills. She considered herself an accomplished accountant and someone who was capable of juggling an enormous workload without any trouble. This new job, though, would have been a test for three *accountants of her ability. And today her boss had the nerve to suggest that she wasn't taking her work seriously enough. Her! Ellen! The woman who takes everything* seriously! *He even intimated that he might need to "make some changes."*

Ellen managed to bear up under her boss's verbal assault and even got through the trip back on the el okay. Now that she was home, though, she lost all reserve. Had she made a mistake leaving

Denver to take this job? Chicago had been good for her in so many ways. She'd learned to be truly independent here, and she discovered how to avoid having people take advantage of her. But she'd come here without family or her closest friends, and when she needed a shoulder to lean on, she really had no one to turn to.

I wish Darla was here, *Ellen thought as she slumped forward, covering her face with her hands. If Darla were around, she would be capable of doing just about anything to make Ellen feel better, whether it was having them run through the snow without their coats, dance ridiculously to the B–52's, or sneak back to her office to rearrange Ellen's boss's desk. Whatever it was—and with Darla, it really was impossible to predict—Ellen would wind up laughing and loosening up.*

Darla wasn't here, though. She had never seen the apartment in Chicago. In fact, they had barely spoken since Ellen left. In the ten years they were best friends, Ellen and Darla had gone through rough patches before. They didn't speak for three months after Darla unwittingly poached Ellen's boyfriend in college, and they went at least six weeks without speaking after Darla forgot to call on Ellen's twenty-second birthday. Then there was the blowup over Darla's moving out without notice from the apartment they shared and the chilly period after Darla left her husband and one-year-old behind to volunteer with the Red Cross in New Orleans and Ellen got stuck with heavy babysitting duties. They always came back together, though, because they loved each other and their lives were better when they were together.

The move seemed to bring their friendship to an abrupt halt. Ellen could barely understand it. She knew that Darla was having trouble with her marriage, and she knew that Darla took her decision to move a thousand miles away personally, but she still couldn't understand why Darla was so stiff on the phone during their handful of early calls or why she simply didn't return her calls the last few times Ellen left a message.

Ellen had lost her best friend, and it felt like a huge part of her was missing. The thought of this on top of everything that was happening at work overwhelmed her. Tears rushed to Ellen's eyes and rolled down her face. She sat on the floor and sobbed.

Until someone knocked on the door. Ellen couldn't imagine who was there because she rarely had guests. Maybe the concierge had a package for her. Slowly, drying her eyes on the sleeve of her coat, she stood up and answered.

And was stunned to find Darla on the other side.

"What?" she stammered. "How?"

"I see you've been working on your vocabulary. That's good," Darla said, striding into the foyer. She dropped her suitcase on the floor and opened her arms. "What gives, sister?"

Ellen moved into Darla's embrace, still not sure how this was happening. Darla didn't have her address—she'd never wanted it.

"Your grandmother told me where you lived," Darla said, as though she'd been listening to Ellen's thoughts. "And she told me that you sounded like you could use a friend. I thought, 'Hey, I'm a friend,' so here I am."

Ellen was crying again, but these tears felt so much better. She gave Darla another hug and then stepped back to look at her.

"You look great," Ellen said with a broad smile.

"Not bad for a woman in couples therapy who's trying to prove to all of the important people in her life that they can count on her, huh? You look pretty good, too. Do you always wear your overcoat around the house?"

Ellen looked down at her coat. She'd been too upset earlier to re-move it. "I was a little distracted when I got home," she said, shrugging off the coat and leaving it on the floor. "Couples therapy?"

Darla sighed. "It's a long story. One of dozens. You tell me yours and I'll tell you mine. I've got all weekend. Scott's taking care of Bette. He actually encouraged me to come out here."

Ellen's eyes brightened. "You can stay all weekend?"

Darla nodded. "You have ice cream, right?"

"Some. We can get more."

"And you have plenty of red wine."

"Lots."

"Then we're all set."

Darla threw an arm around Ellen's shoulder and they walked into the living room. For Ellen, the apartment had never seemed as much like home as it did in that moment.

Best Friends: The Ultimate Friendship

What is best friendship really? Is it about shared interests? Being on the same team at work? Double-dating? Marrying brothers? Is it something beyond just consistent, mutual, shared positive emotion? Darla and Ellen certainly lost their mutuality, then their consistency, then their sharing, then even their positive emotion. As we've discussed, missing even one of these can cause the rest to come tumbling down. But best friendships go beyond the master checklist. There is some sort of glue that keeps best friends together through thick and thin, through fights and small betrayals, lies and temporarily bad behavior. It has something to do with having opposite but complementary KWML personality styles as well as having the teamwork that leads to personal growth maturity. There is an unbreakable bond in friendships of opposites on the KWML

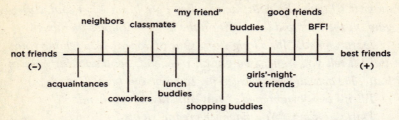

Spectrum of Friendship Quality and Maturity

This spectrum parallels the degree of maturity of character and personal growth two people have reached, and to what extent they mutually share in that maturity. We tend to attract friends of a maturity level similar to our own. People are never the same "age" psychologically as they are outside, "biologically."

map and, with solid personal boundary skill, a commitment to each other not unlike that of marriage.

If you remember our scale of maturity that correlates with the quality and degree of friendship, you will see something remarkable in best friendship.

A best friend is someone with whom we have reached a very high level of maturity. That means that we have good boundaries (which promotes consistency), constructive, win-win behavior toward one another (which promotes mutuality), mature communication ability and politics (which promote sharing), and the emotional ability to be both assertive and courageous (which promote positive emotion). Very importantly, this also means we are frequently using the Cool Eye to monitor our behavior and progress in life.

The solid personal boundaries we have are an absolute requirement for our ability to *commit* to others—whether in a romance or in a best friendship. Darla and Ellen found this challenging since they both started out relatively immature. Early in their

The Three Brains of a Potential Friend

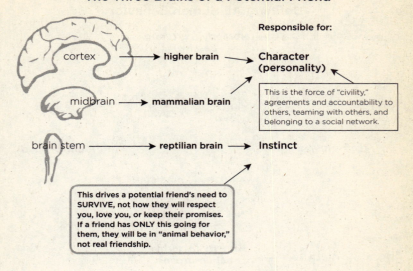

relationship, Ellen and Darla were a bit codependent and had poor boundaries (as evidenced by some of the spats they had). Everything we have discussed so far suggests that this relationship ought to have broken apart long ago. They both had immature personalities, and, as you now know, personality or character results from a connection between the mammalian and higher brains.

Still, sometimes we find a happy randomness in our lives: the soul-mate friend connection that comes about from finding someone opposite to us on the KWML map.

Darla and Ellen were complementary opposites in personality. Darla was a hellion, a wild adventurer full of confidence and not as nurturing as some women are. She was very innovative, imaginative, and creative—a Magician. Ellen was an analytical, soft, gentle nurturer to her friends, a woman who was orderly and more full of well-being than of outgoing confidence—a Queen.

The Cognitive-emotional Spectrums
Defining All Human Behavior

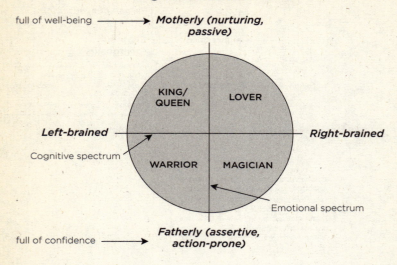

Each woman had intellectual and emotional skills that the other lacked, skills and self-esteem that they had a nearly endless supply of.

Whenever Darla ran her engines too hot on her adventures, she could always count on Ellen for some nurturing energy to re-establish well-being. Whenever Ellen faced an anxiety-provoking challenge, she could count on Darla to charge her up with some outgoing confidence. In this way, they were always assured of loving each other, providing the other with the kind of self-esteem lacking. And they did this from their authentic, most natural selves.

Likewise, on the intellectual side of things, whenever Ellen got too boring and overly analytical, Darla easily shook her out of her left brain (in the higher brain) with some wild and crazy scheme to travel together, run in the rain, or simply laugh. When Darla got too disorganized and random, forgot to pay bills, or monitor her marriage, Ellen brought her back to the logic and order of the left brain to find balance again and better success at reaching goals. Once again, both women had a natural and endless supply of their native style of intellect.

Together, they were *potential* soul-mate friends, full of enough personality, emotion, and thought that could form a fully functional, happy, successful team of "two against the world." Whether they were *destined* soul-mate friends was of course a matter of how willing they were to grow more mature together.

Queens paired with Magicians, or Warriors paired with Lovers, may go through all kinds of boundary conflicts and codependence, inconsistency, and the lies, broken promises, betrayals, projections, perfectionism, and denial that boundary holes engender. They may have periods of win-lose or destructive behavior between them, the fights that show our lack of mutuality. They may be separated by long distances, communicate poorly, and fail to share together. And when under huge stresses—hurt from unintentional ignorance or the loss of a marriage, a job, or one's health—they may even fall into negative emotion for a while. In other words, they can act like reptilian-brained animals at times and lack the civil, higher-brain functions without which they cannot be truly committed to one another. However, in the complementary opposite personalities of the KWML map, they have a kind of glue that keeps them bound potentially even if all four pillars of the master checklist have fallen down.

This is perhaps the only exception to the rules of the master checklist. A true soul-mate friend can make us grow even when we are at our worst. The reason for this is that we draw ourselves naturally toward the center of the KWML diagram, the place of balance, maturity, and psychological integration.

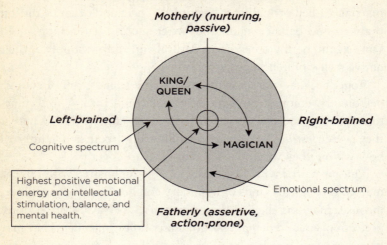

The Cognitive-emotional Spectrums Defining All Human Behavior

Motherly (nurturing, passive)

KING/ QUEEN

Left-brained — Cognitive spectrum

Right-brained

MAGICIAN

Highest positive emotional energy and intellectual stimulation, balance, and mental health.

Emotional spectrum

Fatherly (assertive, action-prone)

Where we run into trouble is when there is pathological narcissism in the best friendship. This is like being a child in an adult's body. It carries with it a lack in all the resources of the higher brain: no boundary skills; destructiveness or win-lose thinking; imbalance of intellectual and emotional management (vividly portrayed by an imbalanced position away from the center on the KWML diagram); minimal conscience and intuition; and, of course, a life spent mostly in reaction, unconscious and going on instinctive reflexes rather than having the Cool Eye turned on to and steering your life.

The self psychologists coined terms such as *true self, false self,* and *ideal self.* Anyone who observes a child will not only see some

The Cognitive-emotional Spectrums
Defining All Human Behavior

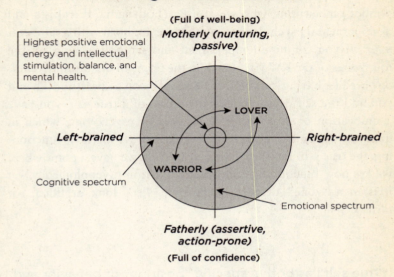

Highest positive emotional energy and intellectual stimulation, balance, and mental health.

(Full of well-being)
Motherly (nurturing, passive)

LOVER

Left-brained ———————— *Right-brained*

WARRIOR

Cognitive spectrum

Emotional spectrum

Fatherly (assertive, action-prone)
(Full of confidence)

imbalance in the use of their bodies but also imbalanced psychological features on the spectrums. When we are young we are all either more of one thing or more of its opposite. In fact, we are usually *very* imbalanced. We are very naive (lacking intuition), or very shrewd and manipulative (lacking conscience), very soft, nurturing, and unconfident or overly outgoing and not so tender, very open to the ideas and feelings of others (holes in the boundary, dependent) or very closed to the lives of others (walls in the boundary, overly independent).

What the self psychologists said more than forty years ago is that we all seem to have a "home base" in life, a kind of imperfect authenticity, and that we grow from this starting point. Jungian psychologists in the meantime say that we start in a role or with a symbol representing who we are. Psychodynamic therapists and developmental psychologists say that we are born with a *temperament.* If you combine temperament and symbolism, you get the four zones of the KWML, which in the terms of quantum psychology are like having "waves" of personality on a spectrum. Then if you add the self psychologists' definition of a true self, you have a unification of three different schools of psychology, which in quantum terms also gives us a point where we are now functioning: the true self. Put this all on a graph and we have a point where we are now functioning and usually function psychologically, yet it is in a "zone" of personality style. Let's look at Ellen, for instance:

"True self" as both a specific "position" of behavior and occupying a zone, or "spectrum" (quantum psychology).

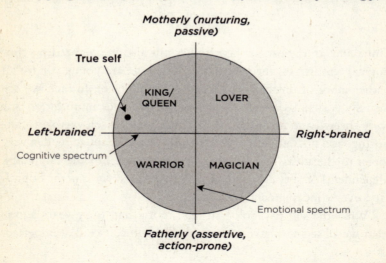

Sometimes in her relationship with Darla, Ellen would get jealous of Darla's prodigious skills at being creative and outgoing and would imagine herself to be just as creative and outgoing (which she is not). This is called putting on a "false self" by the self psychologists, and putting on a "persona" by the Jungians.

Now, in this position, Ellen and Darla would fight bitterly. Darla would call Ellen "fake" and she would be right about that. This is because Ellen pretended to "jump" across the center of the circle, where health is, in an effort to imitate her opposite temperament. She is only pretending to be a Magician-style personality when she is in fact a Queen. This was annoying to them both because it offered no new value to the friendship—both were being "Magicians" at the same time. Where was the balance and

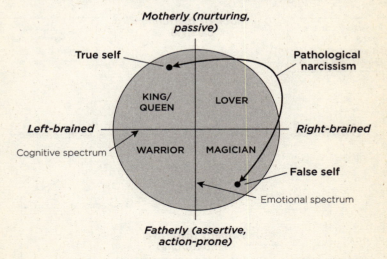

"False self" as "pretending to be the opposite of what you really are" (pathological narcissism).

mutuality in growing toward the center where emotional happiness and intellectual success are?

Putting on a false self was also exhausting for Ellen. She would eventually tire of trying to be wildly creative and confident without doing any real work to cultivate those skills. Likewise, Darla would feel competitive with her and annoyed that Ellen wasn't as giving of her natural, authentic, analytical, nurturing self. They needed to find that it was easiest (and the lowest energy expenditure) to be your true self. They could take examples from each other's natural skills, and then do the mature, patient work of building their *own* skill without codependence on the other friend. This was finally what their year and a half apart from each other forced them to do. They stopped the falseness and codependent reliance on each other and looked inside to do their own work on themselves.

Growth and maturity of personality = the "slow road" from the "true self" toward the real. Adult skills of "ideal self" are a balance of all four.

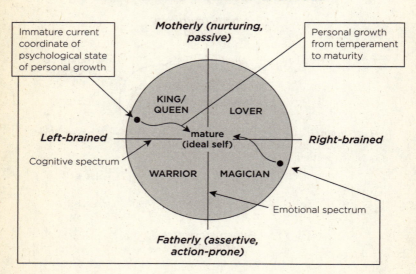

This is how best friends with soul-mate friendships manage to get through difficult situations and mutual immaturity. Since they are opposites on the diagram, even when they are far apart in psychological function, when they take a break and work on personal growth alone and without codependence, they come closer enough to the center that they get comfortable again being their authentic true selves and can "pull" on each other through the influence of friendship. Taking your time this way, growing patiently toward the maturity of psychological balance at the center of the circle, stimulates growth in the skills of the higher brain: boundary skill, constructive win-win mutual behavior, wisdom (conscience and intuition in balance), the well-being and confidence that make happiness, and the left-brain and right-brain skills that lead to the best success at getting to shared goals. In fact, many soul-mate best friends eventually take on a team effort together, like starting a company or founding a volunteer organization.

You might say that maturity level parallels how masterful we are in each of the three brains.

When we are run nearly exclusively by the impulsive, instinctive reflexes of the reptilian brain, we essentially use our unconscious to get along in life. We appear to others to be like adolescents,

Spectrum of Friendship Quality and Maturity

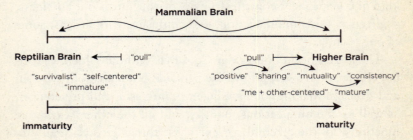

regardless of our biological age. Our behavior is essentially on autopilot, and we "act out"; that is, we act out our unconscious impulses in outer behavior. There is none of the Cool Eye of the higher brain in operation at this level of maturity, and we are only capable of self-centered friendships of convenience.

As we get a little more mature, we learn to get in touch with our mammalian-brain emotions. We are a little more conscious and awake to the social world around us (meaning our Cool Eye is in use a little more, at least enough to think to ourselves "I feel sad" or "I feel scared" or "I feel happy; this is nice"). At this place, we appear to others to operate at the level of a young adult, regardless of our biological age. We start to express emotion and can for the first time bond with others in a more durable way that is a requirement for real friendship and loving others. For the first time, we can have average friendships that are more than just friendships of convenience. We are involved for friendship's sake itself, not some social survival need or reproductive urge. Unfortunately, most of our friendships in life reach this casual level only. With friendships per capita falling in the West in the last twenty years, we are lucky to have a handful of average friends (or even codependent ones), let alone a true best friend.

Codependence is a very relevant word here, because without the boundary maturity of the higher brain, we are left with merely nice emotional connections to others that are likely to lapse into a kind of codependent control struggle, privacy invasion, bossiness, negligence, miscommunication, and confusion with at least some of our friends.

The higher brain houses our Cool Eye, without which we cannot change or grow. It houses the personal boundary, our wisdom and decision making, our intelligence, interests, and preferences, as well as communications, politics, and all the other "executive functions" of the cerebral cortex. These things give us quality in friendship through our own mature character.

Remember, *character is destiny*, and friendship is the vehicle through which its power works in our lives to bring about a happy, successful destiny. If mature character always and without fail leads to quality friendships—even to the pinnacle we call best friendships—simply by working on our character we automatically become human "best-friend-making machines."

Imagine that inside your boundary you are working on your character. You have many connections to people, but you notice that they always seem to be low-quality friendships. They are full of envy, betrayal, and inconsistency. They are one-sided and generally do not make you feel happy. Most of them are friendships of convenience.

These then tend to hover in a state of questionable value to your life—taking up your time, energy, and money—or they soon fail, leaving you socially at square one. This is your destiny. Unhappiness and failure are the direct result of your lack of higher-brain skills and KWML match with others. This tends to extend to the rest of your life. There is higher- or lower-quality friendship in your family relations, in connections with your coworkers and boss, with your clients and business contacts, with the lady at the checkout counter, and with the house painter you see only once every two years. The physical world is composed of atoms, but the social world that we live in—the one that is living and breathing and full of invisible spirit that makes our lives worthwhile—is made entirely of friendship.

What if you could change your destiny by changing your character, bit by bit? What if one small change in the way you conduct yourself could be magnified by a multiple of twenty? What if it wasn't just the addition of friends we were talking about but an exponential ripple of your character through multiple tiers of people?

As you can see, the simple, one-at-a-time changes we make in our character can ripple out not just to our closest tier of friends

Spectrum of Friendship Quality

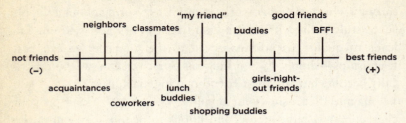

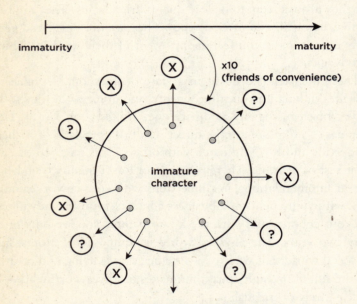

Lost friends or questionable friendships
Destiny: UNHAPPINESS AND FAILURE

but exponentially further into several tiers of people, until we have affected people that perhaps we haven't even met yet. We do so with the same strength of a face-to-face meeting, for there is no more powerful testimonial to others than the reputation we have built with our immediate contacts through our level of self-esteem,

Spectrum of Friendship Quality

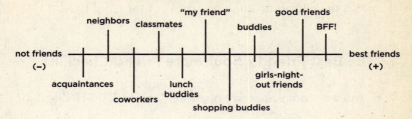

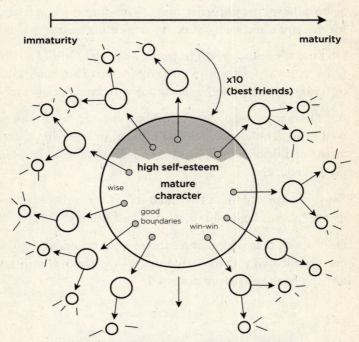

Multiplication of best friendships into notoriety,
even celebrity, through high character.
Destiny: HAPPINESS AND SUCCESS

wisdom, strength of mature boundaries, win-win mutuality, and, of course, the self-observation or "cool" of the Cool Eye.

The Best Friend / Soul-mate Friend Checklist

- Are we "complementary opposites" on the KWML diagram?

- Do I have my Cool Eye turned on? Do I monitor myself against the master checklist, use it to monitor my best friend for the same, and take corrective steps if necessary?

- Do I usually allow myself to be my *true self*? Or do I sometimes let my Cool Eye turn off and miss that I am being fake or trying to pretend to be the opposite of how I really am?

- Am I immature in any way? Do I lack conscience, intuition, well-being, confidence, left-brain logic, or right-brain creativity and flexible thinking? Do I have a number of holes in my boundary?

- Do I monitor my life for reptilian-brain "friends of convenience" versus higher-brain mature best friends?

- Do I notice that with mature friends, my friendships grow out exponentially, constantly bringing new friends into my life that have best-friend potential?

Chapter Twelve

Friendship as Your Ongoing Guide

Each friend represents a world within us, a world possibly not born until they arrive, and it is only by this meeting that a new world is born.

—ANAÏS NIN

Our CHARACTER is an exponential multiplier of high-quality friendships or even best friendships. It all starts with simple, singular changes right inside our boundary. If someone had approached you yesterday and said that only one small change in yourself—giving up an addiction, forsaking your tendency toward angry fits, daring to do one single thing you are afraid of, saying no to the one person you depend on most—could possibly lead you from an average life now to a heroic or even famous life in the future, you never would have believed her.

Now I hope you see it to be scientifically, irrefutably true. Friendship is the vehicle of character's expression. Your character most certainly is your individual destiny. Now it is no longer invisible to you. You can literally see it as you see a map, use it as you use a recipe, and live with it as if it is your own skin. Your life will never be the same. The future will be all the success and happiness you can possibly muster in the tiny changes and growth you can begin, in yourself, right now.

Yet where do you go next as a mature woman with cultivated feminine friendships? The role of friendship is your guide. It will lead you toward a rich individual life among friends and help you become a woman who makes a mark on the world. The deep, symbolic insight in the tales of the ancient Greeks is a key to the role your sophisticated brain wiring takes in having an impact on a complicated social world.

Your understanding of friendship is also a guide to growth beyond mature character. The skills of friendship involve your stewardship of resources, your negotiation of conflicts, and your partnership with powerful others to secure the benefits of all those you share a home with on this planet—the role of Hestia.

My diagrams of psychology, the maps, boundary circles, triangles, and flowcharts, illustrate the processes of your individual mind as a woman. Each of those working parts of your psychology applies equally well to whole groups of people: to companies, communities, and even nations.

Groups are built of individuals, and friendship is the glue that holds them together. If you were to use your newfound skills of friendship to benefit your own life while at the same time giving your excess psychological resources to other women, you would be using this skill to make a real difference in the world. Giving of yourself in this way—to women you don't even know—is in the true spirit of Hestia. Building a successful, happy life is the inborn duty of your reptilian brain, but building a better world is your duty as well.

Make your destiny out of the friendships you grow, and then make it a better world around you.

Bibliography

Barrows, Kate. *Envy*. London: Totem Books, 2002.

Cialdini, Robert. *Influence: Science and Practice*. Boston: Allyn & Bacon, 2001.

Hirshman, Linda R. *Get to Work: A Manifesto for Women of the World*. New York: Viking, 2006.

Howard, Pierce J. *The Owner's Manual for the Brain*. Austin, TX: Bard Press, 2006.

Johnson, Allan G. *The Gender Knot: Unraveling Our Patriarchal Legacy*. Philadelphia: Temple University Press, 2005.

Kindlon, Dan. *Alpha Girls: Understanding the New American Girl*. New York: Rodale Press, 2006.

Kipnis, Laura. *The Female Thing: Dirt, Sex, Envy, Vulnerability*. New York: Pantheon Books, 2006.

Lake, Celinda, and Kellyanne Conway with Catherine Whitney. *What Women Really Want: How American Women Are Quietly Erasing Political, Racial, Class, and Religious Lines to Change the Way We Live*. Washington, DC: Free Press, 2005.

Leon, Vicki. *Uppity Women of the Renaissance*. Newburyport, MA: Conari Press, 1999.

Lukas, Carrie. *The Politically Incorrect Guide to Women, Sex, and Feminism*. Washington, DC: Regnery Publishing, 2006.

Macionis, John J. *Society: The Basics*. Upper Saddle River, NJ: Prentice Hall, 2002.

Paul, Marla. *The Friendship Crisis: Finding, Making, and Keeping Friends When You're Not a Kid Anymore*. Emmaus, PA: Rodale Press, 2005.

Robbins, Alexandra. *Pledged: The Secret life of Sororities*. New York: Hyperion, 2004.

Russell, Bertrand. *The Conquest of Happiness*. New York: Horace Liveright, 1930.

Shlain, Leonard. *Sex, Time, and Power: How Women's Sexuality Shaped Human Evolution*. New York: Penguin Books, 2004.

Trimberger, E. Kay. *The New Single Woman*. Boston: Beacon Press, 2005.

Walker, Barbara G. *The Woman's Dictionary of Symbols and Sacred Objects*. San Francisco: HarperSanFrancisco, 1988.

Watters, Ethan. *Urban Tribes: Are Friends the New Family?* London: Bloomsbury, 2003.

White, Emily. *Fast Girls: Teenage Tribes and the Myth of the Slut*. New York: Berkley, 2002.

Wright, Robert. *The Moral Animal: Why We Are the Way We Are: The New Science of Evolutionary Psychology*. New York: Vintage Books, 1995.

Yager, Jan. *When Friendship Hurts: How to Deal with Friends Who Betray, Abandon, or Wound You*. New York: Fireside, 2002.